The New Life in the Spirit Seminars: Team Manual

Catholic Edition 2000

The New Life in the Spirit Seminars: Team Manual

Catholic Edition 2000

I am the first and the last, the beginning and the end. To anyone who is thirsty I will give the right to drink from the spring of the water of life ... Come, whoever is thirsty: accept the water of life as a gift. (Rev. 21:6, 22:17)

National Service Committee
Chariscenter USA
P.O. Box 628
Locust Grove, VA 22508-0628

We wish to thank the staff of CHARISM, the people of the Diocese of Rockville Centre, New York, and the National Service Committee for their part in revising and testing this Catholic Edition 2000.

Based on *The Life in the Spirit Seminars: Team Manual* developed by The Word of God, Ann Arbor, Michigan and published by Servant Publications, Copyright 1973, 1979. Used by permission of the publisher.

LIFE IN THE SPIRIT SEMINARS is a registered trademark of the Word of God. Used with permission.

Excerpts from the English translation of the *Catechism of the Catholic Church* for use in the United States of America Copyright 1994, United States Catholic Conference, Inc. – Libreria Editrice Vaticana. Used with permission.

Scriptures are from the *Good News Bible with Deuterocanonicals / Apocrypha*, Today's English Version Copyright 1993, American Bible Society, New York. Used by permission.

Contents

DIOCESE OF ALEXANDRIA

2618 VANDENBURG DR.
P.O. BOX 7417

ALEXANDRIA, LOUISIANA 71306
(318) 445-2401

OFFICE OF
THE BISHOP

November 1999

My dear brothers and sisters in the Lord,

The Third Millennium of Christianity is seen by John Paul II as a "springtime of grace" for the Church. God continues to pour out his grace upon his people. What the Holy Father is calling for us to do is to become more aware of this work of God and to respond more effectively to it.

One of the graces God has given his people over the past two millenniums is the grace of Pentecost: the gift and gifts of the Holy Spirit. From the baptism of Jesus in the Jordan to the anointing of the 120 in the Upper Room on Pentecost to the conferral of Baptism and Confirmation on those who believe in Jesus, the Holy Spirit has come to sanctify, to anoint and to empower all for the work of the Kingdom. Unfortunately, for the most part many people who have already been sacramentally initiated into the life of the Church are not aware of this grace within them, which waits to be stirred up anew.

The Life in the Spirit Seminar is one way God has used to re-evangelize his people in this most important truth of his revelation. By walking people through the plan of God for salvation and sanctification, empowering and witnessing, hearts have been enlightened and lives transformed. The message is simple and clear, revealing and convicting, exciting and challenging.

I am happy to endorse this Catholic Edition 2000 of the New Life in the Spirit Seminars. I have seen the power of the Spirit in the lives of those who came to an awareness of the truth of God's Word, and I believe that those who seek God's fuller plan in their life will experience the same through these Seminars.

With personal good wishes, I remain

Sincerely yours in the Lord,

+ Sam D Jacob

Most Reverend Sam G. Jacobs
Bishop of Alexandria

Introduction

It was in the early seventies when I participated in my first Life in the Spirit Seminar. The "manual" was a fistful of purple mimeographed sheets, and Catholics were still getting used to saying "Holy Spirit" instead of "Holy Ghost." It is interesting to note that Webster's Dictionary defines a ghost as a "the seat of life or intelligence" and a spirit as the "breath" which gives life. Since that time millions of Catholics have taken this seminar and have discovered for themselves that the Holy Spirit is not an unreachable, ethereal intelligence, but the very breath of our lives as followers of Jesus Christ. Since the nineteen seventies the Life in the Spirit Seminar has been very widely used throughout the world. It has been translated into many languages and used by many types of groups from a variety of backgrounds.

The original Life in the Spirit Seminar was designed for a very evangelistic situation. It was developed in a community that evangelized people at home, at work, and in social situations, not primarily in church contexts. Those who came to the seminar were from a great variety of spiritual backgrounds. The seminar was designed as a tool to reach a wide range of such people. Many others, however, used the seminar in situations that could best be described as church-renewal situations. The seminars were given in parish or other church contexts. They were used primarily to bring church members to a fuller experience of life in the Spirit, and to redefine the baptismal life that we are given in Christ Jesus, but often need to ratify as adult believers.

In either case, the Life in the Spirit Seminar has an evangelistic character. It is designed to proclaim the basic message of Christianity so that those who hear it can make a renewed commitment to the Lord allowing them to experience a fuller life in the Spirit. The goal is the same as what the *Catechism of the Catholic Church* describes as "the heart of catechesis" which is "to reveal in the Person of Christ the whole of God's eternal design reaching fulfillment in that

Person." (CCC, no 426) The seminar is not designed as a course in adult education or as a theological update on the charismatic renewal, but as a tool for faith formation. In the 1960s the Second Vatican Council called for the renewal of the spiritual life of the Catholic people. It is hoped that the Life in the Spirit Seminar can be an instrument for that spiritual renewal and part of the answer to Pope John XXIII's prayer asking us to pray: "Renew in our day, O Lord, your wonders as in a new Pentecost."

As of the year 1999 we can say that over 60,000,000 Catholics throughout the world have participated in this seminar or variations of it. Our hope is that they have experienced a call to respond to the basic message of the Gospel, and an inspiring vision of what it means to live baptism in the Holy Spirit. We have so much to learn about this ongoing immersion into God's life and Spirit. There is a church in Melville, New York that features a two-tiered marble baptismal font with running water. The refreshing sound of water spills over into every event, every moment of the day, every Eucharist. It is a most striking and pervasive reality, but then so is Baptism. The Spirit flows on and on, dancing over the stones in our hearts, providing the background and foundation for God's Word, God's love, God's presence in our lives.

The seminar is one answer to a need for renewal and evangelization as the Church dwindles in size and in the level of participation. We need evangelistic teaching that centers on the commitment to Christ as it is lived out through his Spirit. We need evangelistic nourishment and a formation process for those who are "quasi-catechumens" living on the borders of faith. The seminar is appropriate for several categories of people who are referred to in the *General Directory for Catechists* as "non-believers, those in religious indifference, those who choose the Gospel, and those who need to complete or modify their initiation into the Christian life." (no 47-51) It is a tool for "beginners" of all kinds. Many parishes and groups have also used the seminar to offer people a new beginning during the traditional penitential seasons of Lent and Advent. Because it is a tool for spiritual formation, the seminar works best when it is presented over a seven or eight week period.

The present revision of the seminar is presented from a sacramental point of view, with the goal being a renewal of Baptismal Vows and a new release of what the Spirit has given in the Sacraments of Christian Initiation. Conversion is presented as a life-long process with possible peak moments. Participants in the seminar are offered the benefits of sponsors, faith-sharing groups (versus discussion), and a view of charisms and gifts of the Spirit as tools for service in the normal life of both the individual believer and the faith community. For a more detailed description of the goals of the present revision please see Appendix D.

Since the Seminar was written, the Church has experienced the renewal of the RCIA (Rite of Christian Initiation of Adults) and we, as Church, are challenged to re-examine the spiritual formation of large numbers of Catholics. In doing so, many of us realize that we need basic tools for adults seeking Sacraments of Initiation (Baptism, Eucharist, and Confirmation). We need tools for parents bringing their children for sacramental gifts of faith that they themselves are unclear about. We need tools by which people can become mature disciples. The Life in the Spirit Seminar is just such a tool, whose purpose a pastor named Fr. Timothy once affirmed when we offered to do a seminar in his parish. "By all means!" he said, "Let the Spirit loose!" So let us imitate Jesus, who even though he was conceived by the Holy Spirit, sought a greater outpouring of that same Spirit again and again, until finally death itself was conquered by the very breath, the fire, the light, the Lord and Giver of Life. "Come Holy Spirit, enkindle the hearts of your faithful."

Therese Boucher

The Feast of the Baptism of the Lord
January 2000

Icons Used In This Book

To aid in using this Manual, small eye-catching
pictures—icons—have been placed in the margins.

This icon alerts you to the Goals or hoped for
results of the Seminar or session

Alerts the reader to information important for
the Team presenting the Seminar

Signals the outline of the Presentation

Flags the "Comments on the Dynamics" for the
team members

Signals the "Expanded Outline of the
Presentation"

Introduces "Comments on the Presentation"

Helpful Resources

PART I:

THE WORK AND GOALS OF THE LIFE IN THE SPIRIT SEMINAR

The section on the work and goals of the 1979 edition of the Life in the Spirit Seminar opens with this reminder from St. Paul: "Using the gift that God gave me, I did the work of an expert builder and laid the foundation, and someone else is building on it. But each of you must be careful how you build. For God has already placed Jesus Christ as the one and only foundation." (1 Cor. 3:10-11)

Paul thought of himself as a craftsman, a skilled worker in the service of the Lord. In order to serve the Lord as an apostle, he had to acquire certain skills; he had to learn to work carefully. He was a person whom the Spirit led with specific guidance and instructions. He experienced the Lord working signs and wonders through him, but still he needed to learn more. He had to learn to build well in order to build up God's temple, the Christian community in Corinth.

The image of a builder is used often in Scripture and is a helpful one for those involved in offering the Life in the Spirit Seminar. In the thirty-fifth chapter of Exodus, Moses told the people of Israel how the Lord had prepared craftsmen to work on his sanctuary. God had chosen Bezalel and "filled him with his power and given him skill, ability, and understanding, of every kind of artistic work for planning skillful designs and working them in gold, silver, and bronze; for cutting jewels to be set; for carving wood; and for every other kind of artistic work." (Ex. 35:30-35)

The image of a temple or dwelling for God is also used in Peter's Epistle. We are reminded that Jesus is the cornerstone and we are like living stones, "a chosen race, a royal priesthood, a consecrated nation, a people set apart to sing the praise of God who called (us) out of the darkness and into his wonderful light. Once you were not a people at all and now you are the People of God." (1 Peter 2:4-10, JB)

The Lord is still working to build his Church today, in the same way that God worked to build his tabernacle, or the Christian community at Corinth. It is the same Holy Spirit who will give us the ability and understanding we need to build up the people of God. An important point to remember is that when we use a tool like the Life in the Spirit Seminar, we are artisans and builders working with living stones. Therefore we must rely on the Holy Spirit, who is the soul of this endeavor, knowing that God will give us all the spiritual skills to work at renewing the Church.

Part I (A) Seminar Sessions

The Life in the Spirit Seminar is designed as an evangelistic tool, a formation experience, and an introduction to a life lived in the power and presence of the Holy Spirit. The eight weeks of sessions help participants realize the fire, the breath, the gifts, fruits and the charisms of the Spirit. Although we receive the life of the Spirit through the Sacraments of Initiation—Baptism, Confirmation and Eucharist, many of us need to fan this spark of life into flames. The Seminar invites us to gather and prepare for a very personal "Pentecost," a new release or revitalization of the Spirit's presence.

In his great discourse at the Last Supper, Jesus made a promise to his disciples: "I will ask the Father and he will give you another Helper, who will stay with you forever. He is the Spirit, who reveals the truth about God. The world can not receive (the Spirit), because it can not see him or know him. But you know him, because he remains with you and is in you." (Jn. 14:16-17)

Jesus knew that when he was no longer on earth, his disciples would not be able to live the kind of life he had called them to by their own strength and ability. He knew that Christians would need a supernatural source of strength, that they would need the strength and power of God himself. So he promised to his disciples the very Spirit of God, and on Pentecost that Spirit came down upon them, to remain with the Christian people forever. The disciples were radically transformed by the Holy Spirit. They were able to preach the Gospel of Jesus in boldness and power. Their words were accompanied by signs and wonders. They drew together to live in new communities, united in one mind and one heart.

The Seminar in a real way echoes both the experience of the Spirit and the preaching of the Gospel that were a part of the first Pentecost. The content and message are what *The General Directory for Catechesis* (published by the United

States Catholic Conference in 1997) calls "evangelistic nourishment," the meat and potatoes of the Good News of Jesus Christ. There are ever growing numbers of people, churched and unchurched, young and old, and from diverse cultural backgrounds in need of such food. Again, the Directory gives us a phrase to describe the Seminar, "initiatory catechesis," a basic brush-up course that can be directed toward: "non-believers and those in religious indifference ... those who choose the Gospel and those who need to complete or modify their initiation (into the Church)." (GDC, 49) For those who are not practicing Catholics, which is the vast majority of those who identify themselves as Catholics today, the Seminar can serve as an introduction to Christ and/or a step towards appreciating the Sacraments of Initiation. For those who are already living a Catholic faith, it offers a fuller understanding of our baptismal life in the Spirit and offers steps for realizing or deepening a vital relationship with the Spirit. In this way we hope to revitalize the Church, to restore the living stones that make up our faith communities.

LIFE IN THE SPIRIT SEMINAR GOALS

As we seek to build the Church, using the Life in the Spirit Seminar as a tool, there are several guiding principles to keep in mind:

1. God offers us a deeply personal and communal covenant with Father, Son and Holy Spirit. We seek to help participants in the seminar to establish, re-establish or deepen an individual relationship with God through Jesus, the Christ.

2. Our Baptism has freed us from sin and brought us to new life through water and the Holy Spirit. We seek to help participants yield to the ongoing presence of the Holy Spirit in their lives. God is active in the lives of believers.

3. As believers we are called to membership in a faith community, and to a life of service using the gifts, fruits and charisms offered through the Holy Spirit.

4. New life means a life of discipleship and growth into Christ Jesus. As Christians we need effective means of growth, such as small faith-sharing groups, prayer, study, sacraments, and the reading of Scripture.

> I ask God from the wealth of his glory to give you power through his Spirit to be strong in your inner selves, and I pray that Christ will make his home in your hearts, through faith. I pray that you may have your roots and foundation in love, so that you, together with all God's people may have the power to understand how broad and long, how high and deep is Christ's love. Yes, may you come to know his love—and so be completely filled with the very nature of God. (Eph. 3:16-21)

The Seminar is based in a vision of the Christian life as "charismatic" by its very nature. Recent studies point out that the reality of baptism in the Holy Spirit, accompanied by a full range of charisms, was a normal part of being initiated and baptized into the early Church. (See the groundbreaking booklet *Fanning the Flame: What Does Baptism in the Holy Spirit Have to Do with Christian Initiation?*) Doctors of the Church, like Hilary and Cyril of Jerusalem, speak about the release of the Spirit as an integral part of the liturgy and public life of the early Church. Hilary of Poitiers (c. 315-367) describes what did and can happen: "We who have been reborn through the sacrament of baptism experience intense joy when we feel within us the first stirring of the Holy Spirit. We begin to have insight into the mysteries of faith; we are able to prophesy and speak with wisdom. We become steadfast in hope and receive the gifts of healing."

The Second Vatican Council called for a broad-based renewal of the rites, teaching, and practices of an earlier version of the catechumenate. Exciting things are happening with the rites and preparation for them. The RCIA—Rite of Christian Initiation for Adults—provides the skeleton for a renewed understanding of the sacraments. The appearance of programs like the Life in the Spirit Seminar can help provide a grassroots understanding of Baptism as a clear, steady stream of spiritual water that sustains us year after year. Many in our Church have been plagued by drought, reduced to watching one small dripping faucet run at a slow trickle; when right behind us, right inside our hearts, is a glorious river with falling, sparkling, cleansing torrents of life, the life of the Spirit.

Let us proceed with every confidence in the Holy Spirit, who will give us the wisdom, love and abilities that we need to build well. We can not be careless and negligent, saying, "The Lord will take care of everything." We can not be lazy, expecting people to return to the Church as if by magic. We can not be afraid of the demands of the Gospel. The Good News of Jesus is our salvation. God wants to take care of his people and we can count on him to do things that are far beyond our powers. The Spirit will give us spiritual gifts and charisms that will help us lead people to Jesus. Prophecy, tongues, healing, and miracles are examples of charisms God will give. So are wisdom, understanding, administration and hospitality. Giving the Body of Christ the necessary skills is one of the main ways the Lord takes care of everything. Helping us use them with the fruits of the Spirit is another.

Participants in today's seminars come with many spiritual, emotional and social needs, but it is better to concentrate on these basic goals and do what we can do well. The Life in the Spirit Seminar focuses on our beginnings, and provides a way for some to start over or regroup before moving forward. Concentrating on a basic commitment to Jesus will give them a simple but profound experience of God. A new found faith will give them a hunger for the things of the Spirit, and a desire to grow and develop in this new life alongside others who are living the life in the Spirit. People completing the seminar usually need help in making connections with additional opportunities for formation, religious education, as well as the life and worship of the sponsoring faith community or parish.

PROGRESSION AND WEEKLY ELEMENTS

The seminar offers a series of talks given by ordinary people, weekly faith-sharing groups, and opportunities for group prayer. Participants are also offered the support of a sponsor (formerly referred to as greeters), and a booklet with daily Scripture readings. Another important element in what is offered is the team itself, made up of sponsors, teachers, and group facilitators. Christians who are experiencing a vital and ongoing life in the Holy Spirit can help others enter into faith. To provide the right kind of contact for the people taking the seminar, there should be one team member for every three or four participants. In terms of content, the first four weeks of the seminar are devoted to the basic message of salvation, and what baptismal life in the Spirit means. People are encouraged to cultivate an effective relationship with Jesus. The fifth week of the seminar is built around the renewal of Baptismal Vows and prayer for a new release of the Holy Spirit. During the final two weeks, the teaching is oriented towards further growth in the life of the Spirit and the call to service afforded by charisms and gifts of the Spirit. Participants are encouraged to take concrete steps in an on-going process of growth and conversion.

EXPLANATION

Many groups who use the seminar offer an introductory session that explains the charismatic dimensions of Catholic faith. This can be a freestanding workshop used to invite people to an imminent Life in the Spirit Seminar. It can be incorporated into an evangelistic service or used as an "eighth" week offered before the other seven.

WEEK 1

The first session offers a simple presentation of God's life, God's unconditional love and the ongoing personal invitation to a relationship with God. The first session also explains the seminar as an opportunity for spiritual formation. A commitment to all the sessions is encouraged, so that the seminar may be most fruitful.

WEEK 2

The second session focuses on the importance of Christ and the gift of salvation. Jesus is Shepherd, Healer, Lord, and Redeemer. Being a Christian and living in the Spirit of Jesus involves committing and recommitting ourselves to a way of life. The presentation explains the basic gospel message and what it means to live as disciples in God's Kingdom. We are presented with the daily choice between good and evil, between sin and redemption. This is a sobering invitation.

WEEK 3

The third session centers on the promise of new life in Jesus. It helps participants realize the goodness of the gift being offered to them. An explanation of how Jesus lived in the Spirit is given. The Baptism of Jesus becomes our model. A witness is given on the place of gifts, fruits and charisms of the Spirit in daily life.

WEEK 4

The fourth session is the week of preparation for commitment to Jesus Christ and openness to the Spirit. This is the week in which the process of conversion is explained as an essential part of the Christian life. This is the week in which people are called to reorient their lives as needed. The presentation explains how to turn to the Lord (repentance and faith) and what is involved in being baptized in the Spirit. In the personal contact with the faith sharing facilitator and/or sponsor, the people in the seminar can work out any problems and receive personal help.

WEEK 5

The fifth session is for renewal of Baptismal Vows and prayer for baptism in the Spirit. People also experience a variety of gifts and charisms that are closely related to a release of the Spirit. The whole session is set aside for prayer.

WEEK 6

The sixth session is about persevering in our baptismal vocation as disciples of Jesus. Participants are challenged to make the decisions and changes necessary to maintain the life in the Spirit, which they have experienced in some way. The focus of the presentation is on prayer, community, Scripture, sacraments and service.

WEEK 7

The seventh session is the final session. It offers a vision of both transformation and mission through the life in the Spirit. The Holy Spirit is at work changing us and enabling us as Church to change the world. As we choose to grow in personal relationships and join ourselves ever more closely to the Body of Jesus we will bear fruit. We must persevere in this work despite trials and difficulties.

Part I (B) The Team

The team itself is an important part of the seminar process. The faith sharing community created among its members becomes a sign and a model of Christian community. Jesus reaches out to the participants through the individual team members and the witness of the relationships within the team. The Life in the Spirit Seminar is an opportunity for Catholics who have experienced a full and vital life in the Spirit to share with others, and to offer a working vision of Christian community. The team becomes a witness to the events of Pentecost and the vitality of the Church during scriptural times and several post-biblical centuries.

The team members are above all witnesses, formed by a passion for evangelization. They are people who seek to live the life of the Spirit in a full and fruitful manner, and who can freely witness to the reality and effectiveness of being a disciple of Jesus. As noted by several Church documents, witnessing and evangelization involve being able to speak about the Gospel in a simple, down-to-earth fashion, and living a life of faith that others can learn from. Sharing our faith is also founded in a real confidence that God speaks and acts through us and is at work in those who receive the message as well. "Evangelization is bringing the Good News of Jesus Christ into every human situation and seeking to convert individuals and society by the divine power of the Gospel itself. Its essence is the proclamation of salvation in Jesus Christ and the response of a person in faith, both being the work of the Spirit of God." (*Go and Make Disciples: A National Plan and Strategy for Catholic Evangelization in the United States*, page 10)

Paul spoke to Timothy about being a servant of the Lord. Paul's exhortation to Timothy is also an exhortation to those who work on Life in the Spirit teams: "Be an example for the believers in your speech, your conduct, your love, faith, and purity ... watch yourself and watch your teaching. Keep on doing these things, because if you do, you will save both yourself and those who hear you." (1 Tm. 4:12,16)

THE TEAM MEMBERS

The 1979 edition of the team manual reminds us of several important qualifications for team members. Paul's instructions to Timothy in 2 Tm. 2:2-10 is used as an example. Paul chose disciples who were, above all else, faithful and reliable. Timothy had to be the kind of person that could be counted on. These disciples had to have the sanctifying gifts, charisms and natural abilities to do what was needed to take care of others spiritually.

Faithfulness includes a commitment to the **vision of renewal** through the power of the Spirit. If a person does not believe in the Good News of the Gospel, the spiritual renewal of the Church, and the individual's renewal in Christ, the team member will be ineffective in the seminar. The team member would not have the motivation to be faithful. Commitment also includes a willingness to do the tasks involved and setting aside the kind of time that is needed. The team coordinator should have clear agreements with team members about attendance and job descriptions before starting the work of the team. If a person does not understand what he or she is being asked to do and is not able to make such an agreement, it will be very difficult for such a person to be faithful as a team member. Roles are—faith sharing group facilitator, sponsor, hospitality worker, teacher and witness.

The team member has to be **sound spiritually and emotionally**. The team member should be living a mature Christian life. People who are not living a good Christian life can not do the work of a team member. Some people need time to grow into spiritual maturity before working on a Life in the Spirit Seminar team. People with serious psychological problems, addictions or emotional disturbances can not do the work of a team member. Pastoral care of other people is not the right therapy for someone who can not yet handle his or her own problems. A lack of spiritual and emotional soundness will show up in a lack of faithfulness to the work of being a team member.

Paul's second qualification is being reliable. This can be applied to an **ability to do the particular tasks** in the seminar. There are many people who are sound and mature in Christian character and committed to the spiritual renewal of the Church but are not able to do the work of a team member effectively. A person needs certain gifts and abilities for the job. Sometimes natural abilities are the underpinnings for charisms—the ability to lead discussion, the ability to speak to a group, the kind of personal strength that inspires respect. But the Lord also gives spiritual gifts and charisms that are really very important—the ability to speak of the Lord in a way that inspires people and a discernment of an individual's spiritual condition and relationship with the Lord. Team members also need a wisdom and understanding of another's personal needs, and an ability to pray with others for healing.

In the twelfth chapter of Romans, Paul writes about people who serve the Lord: "And because of God's gracious gift to me I say to every one of you: Do not think of yourself more highly than you should. Instead, be modest in your thinking, and judge yourself according to the amount of faith that God has given you. We have many parts in the one body, and all these parts have different functions. In the same way, though we are many, we are one body in union with Christ, and we are all joined to each other as different parts of the one body. So we are to use our different gifts in accordance with the grace that God has given us." (Rm. 12:3-6)

A good Life in the Spirit Seminar team can not be developed unless we accept the teaching of Paul that the Lord has not given any one person the gifts and charisms to do everything. That does not mean that one Christian is better than another. But it means that each member has a different place in the work of the whole body of Christ. Some people are good candidates for a Life in the Spirit Seminar team, but many others should seek other opportunities for ministry within the local church.

It is true, the most common problem we will face today

is not people thinking too highly of themselves, but rather people being too fearful. Often people are afraid to work on Life in the Spirit Seminar when the Lord has actually given them the necessary talents and charisms. They have to understand that "the Spirit that God has give us does not make us timid; instead, his spirit fills us with power, love, and self-control." (2 Tm. 1:7) One of the strengths of the approach is that a team is like an orchestra that brings together complimentary gifts, and we must see our own abilities and charisms in relation to others' gifts. A **respect for all kinds of charisms** also involves a personal openness to gifts and charisms needed for the building of the Church. This openness is often seen in peoples' attitude toward the gift of tongues since it is seen as a most unusual charism. It is very difficult for someone who is not comfortable with the gift of tongues to help someone else yield to this gift of prayer. Most often it is the sharing of our experiences with regard to tongues, prophecy and healing that will help another person yield to the gifts, fruits and charisms of the Spirit. As mentioned in the *Catechism of the Catholic Church*, "Charisms are to be accepted with gratitude by the person who receives them and by all members of the Church as well. They are a wonderfully rich grace for the apostolic vitality and for the holiness of the entire Body of Christ." (No. 800)

Every team leader needs to be trained for working in the Life in the Spirit Seminar. The amount of training that an individual needs will depend upon experience and maturity in ministry situations. A person who has functioned as a liturgical or catechetical leader may only need to learn the way the Life in the Spirit Seminar works. On the other hand, someone who is inexperienced in ministry will need a certain amount of guidance. Each person not only needs to learn about the operation of the program, but he or she must grow into maturity in the service of others.

Working in the Life in the Spirit Seminar is a good way to grow in pastoral and catechetical gifts. The experience of helping others lay the foundation for a full and lively Christian life will provide a vision of the importance of an adequate initiation into Christ. The Life in the Spirit Seminar also provides an opportunity to work directly with others and to see the results of his or her efforts in a short-term project. Each person can more easily see if his or her efforts bear fruit. This is also a good way to find out if God is calling a person to work with the RCIA or in adult formation and education.

Today we can add insights from the ministry of adult faith formation and the catechumenate as we work toward initiating people into the fullness of life in the Father, Son and Holy Spirit. Lessons learned in Little Rock Scripture studies, RCIA (Rite of Christian Initiation for Adults), and several excellent alternative Holy Spirit seminars are most valuable. We know more about what needs to be done and can actually name several **different roles** that a team member might have. The four primary roles being—faith sharing group leader, adult teacher (or catechist), sponsor (spiritual friend—previously referred to as "greeter"), and finally, coordinator of the whole process. Additional services include hospitality and set-up. It goes without saying that a particular team member usually does several of these at once, but each is important in it is own way.

FAITH-SHARING GROUP LEADER

- Model participation in worship, prayer, sharing
  - listen attentively, support other team members
- Lead a faith-sharing group after the talks
  - provide a supportive atmosphere for listening and sharing
  - monitor the flow of conversation and participation
  - foster an awareness of God's active presence in our lives
  - provide individual and group prayer as needed
- Help, encourage, and counsel those taking the seminar
  - befriend people through attentive conversations

- Pray for baptism in the Spirit (as well as spiritual gifts and charisms)
- Pray for the seminar and the people in them

Time Commitment
- Attend all team meetings and seminar sessions
- Meet with participants individually during the fourth or fifth weeks (qualified sponsors may meet with some of the participants instead)
- Contact those who miss sessions and offer make-up sessions

ADULT TEACHER AND CATECHIST

- Provide basic teaching according to the outlines for the seminar
- Peview the teaching with the whole team or with a partner
- Include personal examples and witness
- Be willing and able to stay within acceptable time limits

Time Commitment
(in addition to any other responsibilities as a group leader or sponsor)
- personal preparation of one or two talks during the seminar
- time to study a little about the subject being taught
- time to "practice" giving a talk with another team member

TEAM COORDINATOR

The coordinator (or two people who share the role) must have the same qualities as the team member. In choosing a coordinator we are choosing someone who can also administrate a group, provide leadership to a team, and provide an experience of community for all participants. The coordinator is responsible for the seminar as a whole and for the care of the people in it. We need someone who can teach, provide direction, monitor time, and inspire people with a clear and powerful grasp of the Christian life. Once again, Paul provides a glimpse of the gifts, charisms and demands involved in his recommendations for those who "pastor" others (Tm. 3:1-7; Titus 1 7-9). We have listed them as "character" qualities below.

COORDINATOR'S TASKS

• Administrate seminar sessions (timekeeper, and emcee)
• Support and empower others to serve through various tasks
• Overall planning and concern for participants and the whole group
• Present some of the talks and train others in giving talks
• Introduce sessions (especially 1, 5) and conclude them (see 7)
• Care for and form the team, especially by leading team meetings
• Implement evaluation of the sessions and the seminar process

Time Commitment
• a team member with the added responsibility of preparing for the team meetings and talks (ex. choose study materials for team)
• willing to get ongoing training, and be accountable to pastor of sponsoring faith community

Character
• above reproach (of unquestionable integrity), self-controlled
• not arrogant (or presumptuous), violent or quick tempered

- not a heavy drinker (active alcoholic)
- not greedy for gain (not out to make money, not grasping)
- hospitable (a friend to those he or she does not know)
- a lover of goodness, a person of prayer, active in reading Scripture
- sensible (sober-minded, discreet, mastery of self) and reputable
- an apt teacher (capable, qualified to teach)
- manages his or her own household well

SPONSORS AND SPIRITUAL FRIENDS

The 1979 edition talked about **greeters** who "care for participants until they become well established in the Christian life." In the RCIA process people who befriend others in this same spiritual sense are referred to as **sponsors**. Since the renewal of the RCIA in the Catholic Church, we have become aware of the need for spiritual companions along the journey toward conversion. When an adult prepares for Sacraments of Initiation (Baptism, Confirmation and Eucharist) someone from the parish accompanies them through a lengthy preparation period. In much the same way, when adults complete some of the missing pieces of their own formation through the Life in the Spirit Seminar they need someone to be a guide, mentor or friend. Since many in the seminar have needs that are similar to the needs of RCIA candidates, then the name "sponsor" really applies in the seminars too. The sponsor's work is one of the keys to effective evangelization and growth in numbers within a prayer community. Sponsoring others in the Christian life and working in the seminar are two aspects of the same process. It is a pastoral role, based in the willingness to befriend others and involves a real concern for a person's daily life and their response to the message of the Gospel. Much of this support happens naturally as they share their own faith in the small groups and through a weekly phone call to see how a person is doing.

The sponsors themselves should meet the same require-
ments as the members of the seminar team. Some of the
sharing group facilitators may be sponsors as needed. Since
the role of the sponsor may extend for several weeks or
months after the seminar ends, some large prayer communities may want to form a separate team for sponsors with
occasional meetings. Sponsors should take on responsibilities for a definite amount of time (three months is mini-
mal). When they first begin they should have supervision
or training from a team leader or an experienced sponsor.
When a sponsor leaves the team, he or she should be phased
out, and any people whom each one is still responsible for
should be transferred to another sponsor.

The sponsor is not a personal counselor. A sponsor can
sometimes help people with particular problems, but he or
she is primarily a listening friend and a link with the life
of the community, prayer group or parish. Time-consuming
speeches and lengthy attempts to give advice are not usually helpful. Encouraging remarks like, "I know that God is
with you" are appropriate; as is praying with someone for a
moment and surrendering his or her needs to God aloud. It
is important that people reach their own conclusions about
serious needs. A good sponsor lets the participant take the
lead in the depth of the relationship.

SPONSOR'S ROLE

• Welcoming new people into the life of the prayer
  community
• Making them feel at home
• Introducing them to others in the community or parish
  (people they can easily identify with or who could be of
  most helpful)
• Encouraging them to become an active part of that
  community by attending meetings, events and ongoing
  formation programs

- Take a brotherly or sisterly concern for participants
- Keeping regular, friendly contact with them (once during the week)
- Encouraging good habits (regular prayer, Scripture reading, and study)
- Detecting any spiritual problem or other problems that would affect their growth in the Spirit, and either offering assistance with those problems or directing them to available help
- Supplement the work of other team members
  - determine where people stand in an on-going conversion process
  - and in their response to the seminar and the action of the Holy Spirit
  - determine the need for serious change in their lives, taking care to approach any area with the appropriate degree of confidentiality. (Many problems will not be revealed in sharing groups.)

The sponsor's responsibility for a particular person ends when that person is genuinely joined to the life of the community. It might also happen that in the formation of friendships within the group, someone else takes up the responsibility for that person's pastoral care.

Time Commitment
- membership in the same faith-sharing group with participant
- time for a brief phone call or conversation during the week
- a separate time a week or two after the seminar ends for the participant
- to share their overall experience in an informal setting
- time for brief contact with the person for several weeks after

Suggestions and guidelines for sponsoring

1) Contact with participants is normally built into the Life in the Spirit Seminar. Sponsors attend the same sessions and become a part of the faith-sharing groups alongside the one or two in their care.

2) Regular personal contact with these individuals should also be made during the week between sessions, either face to face, or by telephone. If it is possible or practical, invite them to spend some time with you; offering an informal relationship of love and trust is the goal.

3) People in the parish community or prayer group who were the participant's first contact with the faith community or who helped them begin the seminar are natural sponsors. Generally, it is good for a husband and wife to have separate sponsors.

4) Pray for the people you are sponsoring.

5) Be persistent and gentle in offering encouragement. You need not center all of your contacts on spiritual things; casual conversation will often reveal a number of ways that you can help a person's spiritual growth.

6) You may develop a feeling or sense about a problem area that you can not easily define or address. Communicate your concern to someone with overall spiritual responsibility for participants in the seminar.

7) It is normal to feel inadequate or unprepared to care for someone you are sponsoring. God's Spirit is present to help you overcome these feelings and to learn more about this ministry. God will give compassion and both the sanctifying and charismatic gifts of the Spirit.

8) Sponsors may want to study certain sections of *Walking Together in Faith: A Workbook for Sponsors of Christian Initiation* by Thomas H. Morris (Paulist: New York, 1992) and apply them to the Life in the Spirit Seminar.

INFORMATION ABOUT PARTICIPANTS

An effective system of sharing information about participants during the seminar is essential, but needs to be approached with careful attention to confidentiality. The sponsors, group leaders, and the whole seminar team need effective but sensitive ways to work together. If all the team members are sponsors, information about individuals can be shared at team meetings. The 1979 version of the seminar also suggested written reports, called confidential "information transfer sheets," which include: religion, occupation, living situation, and a clear description of what the participant is experiencing. Although sponsors and facilitators need to share a common understanding of a person's concerns, needs, and readiness for individual prayer during the seminar, most teams rely on a much more informal sharing that does not involve written details. If a person drops out of the seminar, either the faith sharing leader or the sponsor should find out why and communicate the reasons to the other. There are many important reasons that we may want to have addresses and phone numbers.

"My friends, if any of you wander away from the truth and another one brings you back again, remember this: whoever turns a sinner back from the wrong way will save that sinner's soul from death and bring about the forgiveness of many sins." (James 5:19-20) God cares about our tendency to "wander."

WORKING TOGETHER AS ONE

The more the Life in the Spirit Seminar team can come together in unity and in love for one another, the more powerful the effect they will have on the people who take part in the seminar. The unity and love of the team will protect the seminar against the work of the evil one, and will be a channel through which the power of the Holy Spirit can touch those participating in the seminar. Such a unity

comes from a oneness in approach, vision and goals as we
bring different gifts and roles to bear in serving the Lord
together. Paul urges us to such oneness:

> That your way of life should be as the gospel
> of Christ requires, so that, whether or not I am
> able to go and see you, I will hear that you are
> standing firm with one purpose and only one
> desire you are fighting together for the faith of
> the gospel ... Your life in Christ makes you strong,
> and his love comforts you. You have fellowship
> in the Spirit, and you have kindness and compas-
> sion for one another. I urge you, then, to make me
> completely happy by having the same thoughts,
> sharing the same love, and being one in soul and
> mind. (Phil. 1:27, 2:1-2)

Behind this kind of oneness of mind and heart lies attitudes of patience, humility, and of self-emptying whereby
team members love one another. Such a unity flows from
our common love for God and for his people, and from a
humble confidence that the Spirit works through us, and
sometimes in spite of us. It is a different model of working
together than what we commonly see in the world around
us. We can take concrete steps as a team to grow our ability to function in love and to become more effective servants in this type of ministry. Our gifts, talents, charisms,
and personal experiences of God will prosper as they are
brought together and polished. Paul reminds us in his letter
to the Philippians:

> Don't do anything from selfish ambition or from
> a cheap desire to boast, but be humble toward one
> another, always considering others better than
> yourselves. And look out for one another's inter-
> ests, not just your own. The attitude that you
> should have is the one that Christ Jesus had: He
> always had the nature of God, but he did not
> think that by force he should try to remain equal
> with God. Instead of this, of his own free will
> he gave up all that he had, and took the nature

of a servant. He became like a human being and appeared in human likeness. He was humble and walked the path of obedience all the way to death—his death on the cross. For this reason God raised him to the highest place above and gave him the name that is greater than any other name.... (Phil. 2:3-9)

The unity and love of the team members for one another is expressed both at the team meetings and at the sessions themselves. It is expressed in real affection that will grow over time. In our contemporary society, we are often unable to freely express our love and support to one another. The apostles frequently urged Christians to hug one another and to show their affection for one another (1 Thes. 5:26, 1 Peter 5:14, Rm. 16:16, 1 Cor. 16:20, 2 Cor. 13:12). It is expressed in speaking words of affirmation and encouragement to one another (1 Thes. 5:11). It is expressed in teaching one another. It is even expressed in admonishing one another to improve, helping one another to see what we have not done right (Col. 3:16). Finally, it is expressed in praying for one another, not just at home, but also together. Love should flow freely among us and be freely expressed if we are to have the spiritual unity and strength that the Lord is offering. Letting the Lord teach us these things is part of growing in spiritual effectiveness as servants of the Lord.

TEAM MEETING

The team meeting is often the only opportunity that members of the seminar team have to discuss their work, but it should also be a time for growth and encouragement. It is important to build unity and faith. If most of the meeting is devoted to administrative details and discussion of the problems, the team will not have the spiritual energy and effectiveness needed to work with participants. Adding study (of a book mentioned in the resource lists) and faith sharing are highly recommended.

PURPOSE
- Create a spiritual unity among the team members
- Provide a place for faith sharing and prayer related to ministry
- Help the team members learn to better serve the Lord
- Communicate about what is happening in the seminar
- Prepare for each new session

FORMAT
- **prayer** for the seminar and the people in them **(10–20 minutes)**
- brief **teaching** that helps members learn how to serve well in the seminar (reading a section of a book about a relevant topic, such as conversion, then asking one another—What does this say about our work? **(10–20 minutes)**
- **faith sharing** about our own spiritual journeys **(10–20 minutes)**
- **business**, such as a review of the last week's session **(30–40 minutes)**
    - discuss any problems that appeared and what to do about them
    - go over the list of people to see how they are doing
    - preview next week's session
    - understand the goal to be achieved and the format

(See the Team Meeting section for individual seminar sessions, but only the business is mentioned for the sake of brevity.)

COMMUNICATING DURING THE SEMINAR

There are several Scriptural models for working together in a ministry situation, especially in Acts. In Paul's second letter to Timothy, we get a brief glimpse at the way that Paul and Timothy worked together. At the end of that letter, Paul speaks about some of the situations and problems that he and Timothy were then facing. He discusses these situations in concrete terms and gives specific instructions about how to handle a specific individual he may encounter. Paul and Timothy worked with the same vision of fostering conversion and worked out the details as they went along.

So too we work at the goals of the Life in the Spirit Seminar as we communicate with one another about each specific situation that confronts us. Discussing incidents that happened last week, the problems that a person in the seminar is having now, the things we need to do in the next session are important. We have to talk about each situation in a very concrete way—"What is John's problem, how is it affecting him, what can we do to help?" We should, of course, talk about these situations in a responsible way, with the appropriate confidentiality. Working toward common goals requires patience since team members themselves will have different expectations and backgrounds. Our own religious experiences color and define what God "should" be doing and how the participants "should" respond.

The goal of our discussion of the seminar at the team meeting is to train ourselves as master builders for Christ. Then we can affirm what we have done well, and change what we have not done well. We have to discuss our work even if it is only instructional, or our work in the seminar will not be nearly as effective. The team must spend a good part of the team meeting discussing what is actually happening and in discussing particular situations.

Our work is in the area of spiritual formation, evangelization and pastoral discernment. These are often new concepts for many on the team. We will be able to help others as we learn to apply general principles to actual situations. For example, we may be working with a person who is timid to open up to the work of the Spirit. We need to be able to have understanding and compassion for someone in this kind of situation and know how to deal with him or her. We need to develop a kind of pastoral judgment, sometimes by discussing these situations in specific, concrete ways, even if there is disagreement among the team members. But we need not fear disagreement; it is a sign that the Lord needs to teach us more about ministry.

Team members can help one another grow in their ability to discern what is happening in different situations. If someone says, "Mary needs something beside prayer for baptism in the Spirit," it is good to ask that person what the grounds for that opinion are. Sometimes a person has a God-given sense about the situation that can not be easily expressed in words. But more often, people can give reasons for the judgments they make, especially if they ask themselves the question: "What things indicate to me that this is so?" If we carefully examine the grounds on which we form our opinions about the different situations and people in the seminar, we will learn to recognize when we have formed our views on poor grounds and will be able to maintain a better perspective on what is really happening.

In order to be able to communicate effectively with one another, team members have to learn how to observe, and describe spiritual needs. Sometimes we even need to learn a common language rooted in a Catholic charismatic spirituality that can be used during team meetings and small group sharing situations. In Acts 19, we have an example of how Paul worked in one situation:

> While Apollos was at Corinth, Paul traveled through the interior of the province and arrived in Ephesus. There he found some disciples and asked them, "Did you receive the Holy Spirit when you became believers?" "We have not even heard that there is a Holy Spirit," they answered. "Well then, what kind of baptism did you receive?" Paul asked. "The baptism of John," they answered. (Acts 19:1-3)

Paul then went on to tell them about Jesus, to baptize them and to pray for them to receive the Holy Spirit. Paul must have realized that though these people seemed to be Christians there was something missing. So Paul asked them a simple question, a question that revealed what the situation really was. He asked them about their Christian past, about what had happened to them. Once they told him about their situation, he knew what to do.

Besides staying in communication with one another, the team members have to stay in open communication with the people in the seminar. Like Paul we have to ask the people in the seminar what is happening to them in relation to the Lord and to the seminar. At first, it may seem awkward to talk about spiritual realities, because such things are private in our society. But remember that we are working with people's personal lives, which is not the same as private. Remember also to give people permission to pass when sharing responses to questions.

Sometimes we can be blocked from finding out people's true situations by a fear of asking them specific questions. We may be afraid that they will be offended. In actuality, people are rarely offended by such questions if we ask them with genuine concern. We may be afraid that when the person answers, a problem will appear that we can not deal with. We need not fear our own inadequacies. The times when we are confronted with questions we can not answer or problems we can not handle are the times to open up and let the Lord teach us what to do.

We can also have a false view of faith that will act as a screen preventing us from seeing what is really happening. People sometimes feel that if we just have faith in the Lord, we can sit back and do nothing and the Lord will take care of everything in the seminar. It is true that the Lord wants us to put our faith in the Spirit and trust God to take care of everything in the seminar, but he does not want that faith to blind us from looking at the situation. Often the way he wants to work is to show us a need and to teach us how to meet it.

Part I (C) Teaching and Dynamics

When Paul described the aim he had when he began to work among the Corinthians, he said:

> When I came to you, my friends, to preach God's secret truth, I did not use big words and great learning. For while I was with you I made up my mind to forget everything except Jesus Christ and especially his death on the cross. So when I came to you, I was weak and trembled all over with fear: and my teaching and message were not delivered with skillful words of human wisdom, but with convincing proof of power of God's Spirit. Your faith, then, does not rest on human wisdom but on God's power. (1 Cor. 2:1-5)

Paul had keen insights about fostering faith that are echoed in Paul VI's *On Evangelization in the Modern World*. **The Holy Spirit is the principal agent of evangelization.** Paul's aim was to cooperate with God as the Spirit worked among the Corinthians. A spiritual change was needed. God had to do something with the Corinthians that no one person could accomplish. What the Corinthians needed is the same thing that people who come to the Life in the Spirit Seminar need—a change produced by a direct working of God. We see something similar in Jesus who chose to be empowered by the Spirit. After his baptism in the Jordan, Mark says that the Spirit drove Jesus into the desert and then into ministry. Jesus and Paul depended on the dynamic intervention of the Spirit. So must we.

"We have confidence in God through Christ. There is nothing in us that allows us to claim that we are capable of doing this work. The capacity we have comes from God; it is he who made us capable of serving the new covenant, which consists not of a written law but of the Spirit. The written law brings death, but the Spirit gives life." (2 Cor. 3:4-6)

The Life in the Spirit Seminars are a work of the Spirit or they are a failure. God makes it possible for us to bring new life to people. And in a very real sense, this gift has already been given many years earlier. We are midwives, and late at that. We can expect the Spirit to be with us and to work in us, and in the people in the seminar. The basis of our service, therefore, is a paradox. We are acting in confidence and faith, but all that happens is a gift beyond our control. As Paul said in his letter to the Galatians, "Does God give you the Spirit and work miracles among you because you do what the law requires or because you hear the gospel and believe it?" (3:2) The answer is clearly, because you hear with faith. We have to know that the power, the love, and the presence of God are available to us. Our faith is in God, both as individuals and as a team. One way we can act on this faith is to begin our work with prayer. The Life in the Spirit Seminar is built with prayer, asking that charisms of intercession, teaching, healing and wisdom be given as we need them. We support the seminar with prayer. We know that God wants to work through us and that God wants to work in the people who come. We know that God is willing to work miracles among us. We know that God stands in our midst.

The second dynamic is a transparent faith. It is essential to the team meetings and the seminar sessions themselves. We must learn to create an atmosphere where people can learn to speak in faith and to act in faith. When we talk about problems in the seminar, we can speak about them in a way that expresses confidence that God will work, or we can speak fearfully and pessimistically. When we speak with the people in the seminar, we can speak to them in a way that conveys our assurance that God is present and will work with them, or in a way that conveys doubt and uncertainty. When the whole group comes together, in our prayer and in our speech, we can create an atmosphere of faith. Or we can allow the seminar to remain lifeless or half-hearted.

Faith comes into our talking and praying with people in the seminar. We believe that God has a very particular love for each person, and we point out the marvels of that presence despite any events or situations. The Lord is offering spiritual gifts and charisms to us. We can expect God to speak through us: in prophecy, in giving us discernment, in facing and overcoming evil, in answer specific prayers when we pray over people, through guiding us in what to say or do, through give us words of wisdom or knowledge, through revealed truths about the situation that we could not know otherwise. The Life in the Spirit Seminar is meant to be open to a broad range of charismatic gifts of the Spirit, in addition to the traditional seven gifts of wisdom, understanding, counsel, fortitude, knowledge, piety, and fear of the Lord. As the *Catechism of the Catholic Church* states, "charisms are to be welcomed with gratitude by the person who receives them and by all members of the Church as well." (No. 800) There are few situations in which God is as eager to make the gifts and charisms of the Spirit available to us as the Life in the Spirit Seminar (or any situation in which we are seeking to reach people who do not know God). We can expect God to give and use the charisms that we need to pray with people. God's power can be present, if we but let the Spirit work through us.

SESSION FORMAT

Each Life in the Spirit Seminar session is made up of a **team meeting** (which is best when held the previous week), **the session itself**: which involves opening prayer, a talk, (a witness), faith-sharing groups, and closing prayer—followed by **supportive services**, like refreshments, book sales and make-up sessions. All of these elements play important roles in the success of the seminar; they should not be viewed as independent of each other, but as an integrated whole.

PROPOSED SCHEDULE for the session would look like this:
  Opening prayer (10-20 minutes)
  Presentation or talk (15-20 minutes)
  Witness about the session topic (5 minutes)
  Small sharing groups (25-40 minutes)
  Closing Prayer (10-20 minutes)
  Refreshments (10-30 minutes)

TALKS

Most of the actual teaching that is done in the Life in the Spirit Seminar is done in the talks. These presentations are short (15-20 minutes), and include three or four important points to make. If the speaker takes care in preparing and presenting the talk he or she can make these points clearly and powerfully, actually helping people to understand and accept them. Usually no one point needs to be developed and explained in detail, just stated in confidence.

Each talk should be prepared with a special consideration for the people who will listen. The speaker should be sensitive to their needs and concerns, stating things in a way they will find clear. He or she should adopt an approach that they can accept, use examples they will understand, and speak in simple, everyday language. **Each main point is illustrated by a personal example.** We can share our faith by talking about events that were touched by God, without making conclusions about our experiences, and without describing every single detail of the event. Think of yourself as a reporter. Examples illustrate how I came to see this point, how I figured out a way to do this myself, what this means to me. Faith sharing not only demonstrates the practical meaning of our teaching, but it shows that the speaker considers these ideas as important in his or her own life.

Speaking from daily life is a way of giving ordinary

people hope about God's love and presence in their lives. Our goal is not to convince people or to settle controversies. We are not offering an analytical or academic perspective on faith or Scripture. We are also trying to avoid criticizing and condemning any people, churches, and religious practices. On the other hand, the speaker should not be defensive or apologetic about the things he or she is saying. An enthusiasm for the subject is contagious and inspiring. The general approach should be: "This is true. It is something great that I have (recently) discovered, and which I share with you."

Remember we can trust in the Lord. God's Word is fruitful and effective. God wants to use us to bless others. Our qualifications are not important, just our willingness to be transparent about our love for Jesus. God will give us the words we need:

"The Lord said to me, 'I chose you before I gave you life, and before you were born I selected you to be a prophet to the nations.' I answered, 'Sovereign Lord, I do not know how to speak; I am too young.' But the Lord said to me, 'Do not say that you are too young, but go to the people that I send you to, and tell them everything I command you to say. Do not be afraid of them, for I will be with you to protect you. I the Lord have spoken!' Then the Lord reached out, touched my lips, and said to me, 'Listen, I am giving you the words you must speak.'" (Jer. 1:4-9)

GUIDELINES FOR TALKS

• Prepare your talk. Pray over it.
    Watch yourself and watch your teaching. Keep on
    doing these things, because if you do, you will save
    both yourself and those who hear you. (1 Tm. 4:16)
• Use normal language, avoiding pious phrases, church
  jargon or charismatic lingo not easily understood by the
  average person (thee, ministry, saved, washed by the
  blood).

- Say what you are saying; it is usually impossible to be too simple or blunt.
- Quote the scriptures, paraphrasing them if necessary to make the point.
- Use examples from your own experience, from other believers or Saints.
- Avoid arguments, controversies, and criticisms of others. "Keep away from foolish and ignorant arguments; you know that they end up in quarrels. As the Lord's servant you must not quarrel. You must be kind toward all, a good and patient teacher, who is gentle as you correct your opponents." (2 Tm. 2:23-23)
- Do not moralize or demand obedience, simply witness to the power of the Lord.

GUIDELINES FOR PERSONAL WITNESSES

(Recommended in explanation and sign-up sessions, and as a five minute follow-up to presentations in each session, especially one and three.)

This involves a brief glimpse of life before a new conversion, how God's love was realized, and what difference realizing God's love makes now. It can be done as an interview also.

- Ask the Lord to give you wisdom and lead you in your sharing.
- Be brief but present highlights of significant changes.
- Mention details of one or two of these changes to arouse interest.
- Talk over your experiences with another team member, watching for what would be most helpful to others.
- Do not be wordy, beat around the bush, include irrelevant details, or emphasize how bad you used to be.
- Do not speak in glittering generalities. Avoid words like "wonderful," "glorious." Do not give the impression that the Christian life is "a bed of roses."

• A witness that follows a presentation should be tightly
focused on the subject of that session.

FAITH SHARING

Coming together in faith-sharing groups is of tremen-
dous importance for the success of the seminar. A warm,
concerned group can set people free to recognize and reflect
upon ways that God has already been present. Then a new-
found confidence in God will free people to respond to the
Lord in new ways, especially if explicit agreements are made
about confidentiality. The facilitator (referred to as a discussion leader in the previous edition) should take special
care to establish this atmosphere of love and interest in the
group. He or she should be warm and friendly, get to know
people and show interest in them by remembering their
names and the concerns they share. Each one should listen
attentively to the things people say, and encourage those
who are timid or shy to share and ask questions. It is not
so much a question of guiding an intellectual discussion, as
it is fostering meaningful conversation. There are sharing
questions for each session designed to guide the sharing.
During the sharing time, the role of the leader is to
direct and encourage. Each facilitator should help keep the
conversation centered on the main points of the talk, but
he or she should also encourage sharing and questions. If
necessary, a particular point can be explained, although
it is more important for participants to share their reactions to what has been said in the talks. **Remember:** If the
group gets stuck on a question it is always appropriate to ask
"What struck you during the talk we just heard?"

Many of the guidelines given above for speakers also
apply to the faith sharing facilitators: sharing from experience,
enthusiasm, not moralizing, avoiding controversies, speaking naturally, speaking in faith. An excellent resource for
facilitators is *Faith Sharing within the Charismatic Renewal* by
Sr. Nancy Keller and Sr. Justin Wirth (Chariscenter USA, 1990).

Of course, one key to successful faith-sharing groups is setting up good groups at the beginning. There are two main principles to be followed here; 1. put each person with the faith-sharing leader who can help him or her the most, and 2. be sure that each group can interact well as a whole. There are some other principles to be kept in mind, although they are secondary to those above. Generally, people can identify best with a facilitator of the same sex, and the leader can spot problems more easily in person of the same sex. Also, many men find a woman faith sharing leader to be an impediment (this is not necessarily the time to confront this problem: first things first).

Spouses should usually be placed in separate discussion groups, although it is best if they attend the same seminar. In separate discussion groups they can often respond more freely to new ideas, but if they are in the same seminar they can also discuss things at home and move forward together.

People who have serious problems, or who are difficult to handle, should not be placed in groups with inexperienced sharing group facilitators. Ordinarily it is best not to put too many people with problems in one group either.

FAITH-SHARING GROUPS

Size
• Each group should have 3 or 4 participants to each facilitator (sponsors for participants are also added to this number).

Purpose
• Help people open up and respond to God's invitation.
• Help them to understand and digest the material presented in the talk.
• Give them a chance to ask questions.
• Allow them to express their thoughts and feelings.
• Provide an opportunity to deal with misconceptions and problems.

- Support them in their efforts to find God in daily life.
- Provide a place for them to begin to experience Christian community.
- See if the talks are being understood.
- Find out how the group is doing.

Format
- The group forms and begins its sharing time right after the talk.
- The facilitator also welcomes questions or the mention of problems.
- The leader begins with prayer, then asks a faith sharing question, and helps people share their responses, without going around in a circle. Monitor sharing time so that no one person dominates or is left out.
- If the group is eager to respond to the talk, each facilitator allows them to share what strikes them. The questions are just a tool. If a serious need arises the facilitator leads a prayer for that person.
- The leader's response to the sharing question would normally come toward the end of the discussion. If the group runs out of steam, be prepared to reread a Scripture from the talk and share what it means to you.
- It is good to conclude with prayer together, especially about things that have been shared.

MAKE UP SESSIONS

The ideal is that each participant should be present for each session, since much of the growth in faith happens over time and through the faith sharing community that evolves during the seminar sessions. There are several needs to consider—the need for a sound formation, the need to be welcomed, and the need for opportunities to grow in faith. If someone misses too many sessions, we should not hesitate to ask that person to start another seminar. When someone misses a session there should already be a plan in place to help that person cover the material. Create guidelines such as, "Missing two sessions indicates that they will get more out of the seminar if they start over." Some groups use audio tapes to make up sessions. Others offer an informal meeting after the general session ends during which someone summarizes a previous session. If a number of people have missed a particular session, we might consider holding a special make-up session. Individual make-ups should usually be given by the person's sharing group leader. If this group facilitator is not also the team leader, he or she could bring a tape of the talk, play it, and then discuss it with the person.

We should not feel that we have to offer make up sessions for everyone. Sometimes we simply lack the resources to do so. In most cases, it is not unreasonable to expect people to make the effort to be at all the sessions. If people with serious psychological or spiritual problems are absent, we should probably be less eager to make up sessions with them, unless we feel that the session or something else we can do will allow us to address the problem. Their absence is probably a manifestation of their problem, and it will manifest itself in other ways further on. On the other hand, people who have the potential to help others might be worth extra effort (not because they deserve it any more, but because in helping them we will be helping many more people).

AUXILIARY SERVICES

One person on the team should be designated as an administrative helper. He or she is responsible for taking attendance, physical set up and refreshments, as well as distribution of literature. Obviously, many more people can help with some of these tasks, even participants, as time goes on. The helper might also be a regular sharing group facilitator.

These auxiliary services may seem minor, but they play

an important part in the successful presentation of the seminar. If the setting is well arranged, people will find it easier to be involved in the seminar, and it will be that much easier for them to turn to the Lord. If the right kind of resources is available, it can further explain the teaching and build people's faith.

Setting
- Arrange chairs to help people see speakers and other participants.
- Circular or semi-circular arrangements are best.
- Large groups may need straight rows with permission to move chairs during small group sharing.
- The room should be well lighted and ventilated.
- There should be a blackboard, white board or newsprint for the speaker's use.

Registration
- A team member should take attendance, especially in a large group.
- Collect a list of people's names and addresses at the first session.
- Use preprinted name tags (if possible).

Hospitality
- Offer a few simple refreshments, foster informal sharing and the building of relationships, and an opportunity for participants to serve by bringing food.

Book Table
- Sell only a few books, tapes and pamphlets that are easily understood. People are more likely to read, if only a few are recommended.
- Making leaflets and books available also teaches people the importance of study and is often an important part of building personal prayer habits.
- Suggestions for the most basic resources are marked with **** in this manual.

HELPFUL RESOURCES

Christian books, bibles, tapes, pamphlets, and other material can be an important help to both team members and participants in the Life in the Spirit Seminar. **A few helpful resources can be given to participants during the seminar, or sold at a book table during the sessions.** Reading levels and motivation will vary widely among participants. Many will find it helpful to begin with pamphlets and leaflets, like those published by Dove Publications. The team should consider purchasing some of the most basic pamphlets and giving them to participants in the seminar. **(ORDERING should be done 3 months in advance.)** Toward the end of the seminar, team members should also help people select reading matter that will help them grow in the Christian life. Many of these **resources can be obtained** from the "Renewed Life" catalogue published by Charismatic Renewal Services 237 N. Michigan St. South Bend, IN 46601. (They can be reached at 800 348 2227.) Another source on the Internet would be www.amazon.com or www.bibliofind.com for out of print books that team members might want.

Each **participant** in the seminar should have the use of a Bible and a booklet or collection of daily Scripture readings such as *Finding New Life in the Spirit: A Guidebook for the Life in the Spirit Seminars* (Servant Publications, 1972). Bibles are helpful for finding the context of a passage used during a session, for prayer and for any additional Scripture readings that the seminar leader may recommend at the conclusion of each talk. Recommended translations include the *New American*, the *New Jerusalem*, the *Catholic Study Bible*, and the *Good News Bible—Today's English Version* (1993). Some people may want to explore the charismatic renewal on the Internet by visiting an extensive site in San Francisco—www.garg.com/ccc/

Helpful Dove **Leaflets** include #1 Baptized in the Holy Spirit, #8 The Gift of Tongues, and # 3, 4, 10, 43, and 46. Dove **Pamphlets** include #201, 202, 217 (Dove Publications, Pecos, New Mexico 87552; website www.pecos.org). A Dove Pamphlet Pack of any eight titles may be ordered.

Booklet: **** *An Introduction to the Catholic Charismatic Renewal* by John and Therese Boucher (Servant Publications, 1994) which provides a brief description of the charismatic movement.

Books that describe the work of God's Spirit include: **** *Still Riding the Wind* by George Montague, S.M. (Resurrection Press, 1994); *As By a New Pentecost: The Dramatic Beginnings of the Catholic Charismatic Renewal* by Patti Gallagher Mansfield (Franciscan University Press, 1992)

Periodicals are *God's Word Today Magazine* (Box 64088, St. Paul, MN 55164) and **** *Pentecost Today* (formerly called the *Chariscenter USA Newsletter*; Chariscenter USA, Box 628, Locust Grove, VA 22508-0628) which can be given to participants for free (during one of the later sessions).

It is recommended that **team members** study and read for their own formation and to enhance their ministry to others:

Baptism in the Holy Spirit: Reflections on a Contemporary Grace in the Light of the Catholic Tradition edited by Francis Martin (St. Bede's Publications 1998)

**** *Fanning the Flame: What Does Baptism in the Holy Spirit Have to Do with Christian Initiation?* Edited by Kilian McDonnell and George Montague (The Liturgical Press, 1991)

Part I (D) Participants and Conversion

Each Life in the Spirit Seminar is made up of more than a series of teachings and the team that presents them. It is made of people, individual people with unique personalities and backgrounds, who have come to us to find out more about the new life that God is offering. They may have come for any number of reasons, from a real hunger for a new life to simple curiosity, but whatever their motivation, each one of them has been entrusted to us by the Lord. God loves them and his earnest desire is to see them receive new life. If our desire is to serve the Lord, our overriding concern must be to give these people all the love and support they need. In his first letter to the Thessalonians, Paul speaks about the way he worked to build up the Christians at Thesalonica.

> We were gentle when we were with you, like a mother taking care of her children. Because of our love for you we were ready to share with you not only the Good News from God but even our own lives. You were so dear to us!... We encouraged you, we comforted you, and we kept urging you to live the kind of life that pleases God, who calls you to share in his own kingdom and glory.
> (1 Thes. 2:7-8, 12)

Paul was a great teacher and preacher. He healed people and worked miracles. He received revelations from God and spoke them to the people. But he did not neglect the work of caring for each person individually, of talking to each one personally, of working to help each one serve God better and grow stronger in the Christian life.

In the Life in the Spirit Seminar we need to care for each person individually. The normal course of the seminar—the teachings, the contact with Christian witnesses, prayer for baptism in the Spirit, support within small faith-sharing groups—is enough in itself to address many spiritual and personal needs. But each person will have other, unique needs that can only be met when he or she is individually cared for, spoken to and helped. We also need an appreciation of the complexities of the conversion process that an individual person is involved in at any particular stage of life.

There are many ways we can give people individual attention during the seminar. Sometimes there are opportunities in the faith-sharing groups to help individuals work out personal problems or apply the Gospel message to their own lives. Sometimes informal contact with people, talking with them for a few minutes before or after the sessions, can make all the difference in opening up to the Lord. Sometimes we need to get together with someone at another time in the week, when we see that they need some sort of further contact or feel that the Lord is leading us to meet with them. **We need to meet with individual people** after the fourth week, when we prepare them for the renewal of baptismal vows and prayer in the fifth week, so we can tailor the way we lead them in prayer

The work of individual attention begins when a person first comes to us, at the very beginning of the seminar. Our first duty to each person is the willingness to develop loving relationships between the individual and members of the community. Within this context, we can help them decide if our seminar is really going to help him or her to develop a fuller Christian life. Many people will come to us with needs that the Life in the Spirit Seminar is not designed to address. Sometimes we will be able to help these people outside of the seminar, but at other times we will not. If we let the Lord teach us how to deal with the different types of people who come to us, we will be able to give each person as much help as we are equipped to give. Most people can benefit by what the seminar has to offer and should be welcomed, then referred to other services in the community afterwards.

Each person is unique, and as we consider each individual we should remain prayerful and confident in the spiritual journey that each one is traveling. There are many ways to look at spiritual needs and the different ways that people handle them. We will learn through our experiences and through the counsel and teaching of the Lord. What we have to offer through the seminar is the opportunity for some very real progress in answering God's call to conversion according to individual needs. We are also fostering an awareness of the gifts, fruits and charisms all of us have received through the sacraments to enable us to choose and serve Jesus. What different types of people will have in common is this invitation to conversion, but response will vary.

> Conversion is the change of our lives that comes about through the power of the Holy Spirit.... Unless we undergo conversion, we have not truly accepted the Gospel... [We] must be converted—and we must continue to be converted! We must let the Holy Spirit change our lives! We must respond to Jesus Christ. And we must be open to the transforming power of the Holy Spirit who will continue to convert us as we follow Christ. If our faith is alive, it will be aroused again and again as we mature as disciples. (*Go and Make Disciples*, page 2)

How people respond to this invitation, or rather the style of their response will vary greatly. It is up to us to offer people the challenge of the Gospel and the patience to let them answer God according to their own situations.

THOSE WHO ARE READY TO DEEPEN OR BEGIN THEIR LIFE IN THE SPIRIT DURING THE SEMINAR

Most of the people who will come to us are in this category and are willing to take another step in their journey. They will usually have some difficulties living the life in the Spirit. These may include: underlying human problems (fears, not wanting to change, lack of spiritual support, inadequate language to express spiritual experiences, resentment towards the Church, etc.). They may have "theological" problems (misconceptions about the "charismatic," putting limits on God's power, lack of adult religious education, moral confusion, or insufficient faith in God's love and promises). Most normal obstacles are taken care of through the seminar.

THOSE WHO ARE NOT YET READY TO MAKE OR RENEW A GENUINE COMMITMENT TO CHRIST AND TO LIVING BAPTISM IN THE SPIRIT

Some of these people are experiencing a genuine lack of faith or an unwillingness to repent, serious theological reservations, or a broken relationship with the Church that needs a sacramental resolution. Our ability to help them varies in each case. If we have the resources to deal with their needs, and they are in regular contact with our faith community, we can offer another course that will bring them to deeper faith, or referral to a pastoral service, before they begin the Life in the Spirit Seminar. Sometimes we can recommend a book, and suggest that they read it and then come to the seminar. But if we do not have any other help to offer and do not have regular contact with this person, then we should consider bringing this person closer to Christ through the Life in the Spirit Seminar.

THOSE WHO COME FROM OUT OF TOWN

In geographic regions where there are many seminars, it is ideal for "out of towners" to attend a seminar in a place closer to home. In this way they will become part of a worshipping community located near them. There is a bonding that can happen during the seminar that makes it harder to become part of another community later on. On the other hand, most people are very mobile in their choice of activities and parish faith communities, and some cities have only a few seminar options. In these cases it is important to help people face this issue of how and where they make spiritual allegiances at some time during the seminar. Greater efforts must be made to help these people discover regional options and resources in weeks six and seven.

THOSE WITH SERIOUS PSYCHOLOGICAL PROBLEMS
There are different types of serious psychological problems and things that we can do for these people. In general, a community has to be fairly mature before it can be of any real help to people with serious psychological problems. The Lord can equip us to help with every problem, but if we take on someone's problems before God gives us the gifts to handle them, we will feel drained and overwhelmed in handling the needs of the larger group of participants in the seminar. If a person is disruptive, unbalanced (i.e., has a history of "breakdowns"), or if his or her behavior is an obstacle to other people in opening up to the Lord, we should ask such a person not to come to the seminar. On the other hand, if someone has a serious psychological problem but can function normally, the Life in the Spirit Seminar will probably be helpful. Wisdom and discernment are needed in these situations.

Jesus can help every person, but sometimes God says to us: "That is not a service that I have given you the gifts to perform." Paul said in Romans, "Do not think of yourself more highly than you should. Instead, be modest in your thinking, and judge yourself according to the amount of faith that God has given you." (Rms. 12:3) We can not help every one in the Life in the Spirit Seminar, and we may occasionally have to tell people that this is not the right place for them. Sometimes that will be because the seminar is not designed to help every person, sometimes because our community, parish or prayer group is not able to help them. God wants to see Christian communities, bodies of Christ, grow up that can help every person who comes to them. But we have to know when we have grown to that point and when we are not yet there, we have to recognize which gifts we have and which we have not received. The leader of the seminar, or faith group facilitator would normally help someone explore other options instead.

THE CONVERSION PROCESS

Each person in the seminar will bring two things when he or she first comes. First of all, each person will already have some faith, even if he or she does not realize it. Jesus said, "No one can come to me unless the Father who sent me draws him." (Jn. 6:44) God has already begun to work in them and is drawing them to himself in some new way at this time. We can have confidence in the power and presence of the Spirit who has been with each of us since the beginning of our existence. We can also trust that God's life has been given through the sacraments. But at the same time, each person brings obstacles that can keep him or her from turning to the Lord—things like personal difficulties, theological questions, a lack of knowledge about Christianity, a life of religious indifference, an incomplete formation as believers. Our main service as Life in the Spirit team members is not to solve all of the problems people have when they come to the seminar, although when we can solve them or give them significant help we should. But our main responsibility is to help and encourage them to have faith in the Lord and to make a new decision to fall in love with God in a deeper way. We are offering the vision of a solid foundation as Catholic believers. Our task is to help them to take a step towards a more vital relationship with Jesus and realize the importance of a complete initiation into the faith and into the Catholic Church.

When we consider each person and the strengths and weaknesses he or she brings to the conversion process, we have to keep our true responsibility to each one in mind. People can have many different kinds of problems, which will not keep them from a new relationship to the Lord. Our responsibility is to see that they are able to face their problems with the same patience and respect that Jesus has for them.

Participating in the Life in the Spirit Seminar will set a process of growth in motion that gives people the tools to overcome obstacles to faith. As people begin to hear and understand God's word through the teaching in the seminar, their mistaken attitudes may dissolve and they will be able to approach the Lord in a better way. The experience of Christian sharing and mutual support in our communities will also make a big difference. Our personal contact with people will be a major help in facing obstacles; witnessing through encouragement, individual prayer, and everyday examples of faith will help them take necessary steps themselves.

This process of growth in the Life in the Spirit Seminar is presented in two parts with a slightly different focus—the first five weeks of the seminar and the last two. In the first five weeks, up to the renewal of Baptismal Vows and prayer for baptism in the Spirit, that process should be aimed at two things. The first is fostering a deeper faith in people, based in an awareness of the ways God has been and is present to them. The second is an inner assurance that the Lord comes to them, is active in their lives and is inviting them to a deeper life in his Spirit. They often experience a real joy in God's promises at some point in these five weeks. In this way, each person becomes ready to ratify their own baptismal commitment to Jesus Christ as Lord. He or she comes to a decision of the heart and mind to follow Jesus and live the Christian life through cooperation with the Spirit of Jesus. A part of this renewed commitment is renouncing serious wrongdoing and taking any essential steps to begin and to continue dealing with obstacles to the Christian life.

It goes without saying that conversion is a life-long process that unfolds in the context of the Christian community and the sessions are addressed to only one of many "essential moments" in the Christian life. It can often happen that a person will have genuine faith that is just a tiny, undeveloped part of his or her life. Also, feelings of doubt can exist at the same time as true faith. Wayward desires and temptations can still trouble someone who has genuinely repented. These doubts, feelings and desires will sometimes blind a person to the realities of what God is already doing in a person's heart. Sometimes we will be able to recognize

God's presence and the spiritual state of someone and help them discern the next step in faith. Our own patience and confidence in Jesus who is the Way and the journey will be both contagious and often challenging.

THE TIMING OF CONVERSION

People do not "catch" faith or come to a decision to follow the Lord more closely during any particular week. Some people come to the seminar well prepared. They are accustomed to prayer and to yielding to God. Some do not reach a point of surrendering to God until team members actually pray with them through the laying on of hands; that is often the moment when they turn to the Lord in faith. We do not need to be anxious about when a change or a decision is made. Sometimes we will be able to see God's actions in the way someone responds to the talks; sometimes we will not. But our ability to discern an individual's spiritual condition is not as important as our realization that the process of growing in faith is going on inside them. It is that conversion process that we serve with gratefulness.

After the fifth week, our concern changes somewhat. We are still concerned with faith, but much more involved with a vision of the concrete ways that faith is lived out within the Christian community. Part of our major concern in the last two weeks is encouraging people to continue, to persevere, to become firmer and more mature in faith and obedience to God's love. If we forget that every Christian has to grow in faith, and needs encouragement to do so, we will be very poor workers in building Christian communities and helping Christians grow. "What we have seen and heard we announce to you also, so that you will join us in the fellowship that we have with the Father and with his son, Jesus Christ.... God is light, and there is no darkness at all in him." (1 Jn. 1:3, 5)

The last two weeks are the crucial time for people in

the seminar to make concrete decisions to connect themselves to a faith community in a way that will allow them to
receive the help they need to grow further in the life of the
Spirit. Living the Gospel message and baptism in the Holy
Spirit are meant to be communal realities. We are called to
live the life of Jesus as part of a local church. As team members we encourage participation in the life of a faith community and/or parish, so that a person will have many levels
of support for growth as a Catholic. We encourage involvement in parish ministries also, since service and growth go
hand in hand as parts of what God is doing. As Paul said in
I Corinthians:

> After all who is Apollos? And who is Paul? We
> are simply God's servants, by whom you were
> led to believe. Each one of us does the work the
> Lord gave him to do: I planted the seed, Apollos
> watered the plant, but it was God who made the
> plant grow. The one who plants and the one who
> waters really do not matter. It is God who mat-
> ters, because he makes the plant grow. There is
> no difference between the one who plants and
> the one who waters; God will reward each one
> according to the work each has done. For we are
> partners working together for God; and you are
> God's field. You are also God's building. (1 Cor.
> 3:5-9)

God is at work in the Life in the Spirit Seminar, drawing
people into the life of his Church. We have just one small
part to play in bringing people into a life of shared discipleship. We do not "get people baptized in the Spirit" or "get
them to the Lord" and then abandon them. We hope to
connect them with a small faith community, but also with
the larger picture of what new and glorious things are possible as whole parishes and diocese function in the power,
healing, and transformation that is in the Body of Christ.
God will give experiences of community through a number
of means that are part of the seminar. We have to make ourselves available to each person as his servants in the part

of the work that we are assigned for the building of the Kingdom. One person may want us to plant a seed, one person may want us to water a plant, or to hoe, or to prune or to do any of a number of things. Our task is to do that which will serve the process of a person's turning to God, and point toward the universal nature of what God does in the Church.

Since the Life in the Spirit Seminar was first designed, there has been a lot of work done to identify the different realities that are a part of a full conversion experience. A recent scholarly explanation can be found in *The Conversion Experience* by Donald L. Gelpi (Paulist, 1998). To simplify what is said, conversion includes several elements. First a religious and spiritual change by which we recognize Jesus in our lives. The seminar is a very fine tool in fostering spiritual conversion. Conversion can also be intellectual and can mean searching out God who is truth. The third kind of conversion is moral and involves what we embody with our whole lives and all of our actions. A fourth conversion is ecclesial as mentioned above and involves choosing a faith community and parish. The fifth is socio-political by which we become involved in transforming society and working for the common good. Any one of these can be a starting point for the others, and can be a part of someone's agenda when they are going through the seminar. *It is not a question of embracing all of them as the aims of the seminar, but of being aware of them and not devaluing any of these ways that God may be inviting someone to make Jesus the Lord and Savior of their whole existence.*

These are some of the conversion problems that can block people from turning fully to the Lord, and may need prayer and attention:

LACK OF KNOWLEDGE—Often people will have hazy ideas about the Christian life or about baptism in the Spirit, or indeed the nature of the Sacraments of Initiation that they may have received. Some may be lacking a religious vocabulary to use when discussing their spiritual experiences. By the fifth week, their ideas should be clear enough so that they can make or renew a genuine commitment to the Father, Son and Holy Spirit. They will often experience a spiritual conversion, but will need to learn more over time so that they can come to an greater intellectual conversion. Study and continued formation are to be encouraged as means of growth after the seminar.

PERSONAL DIFFICULTIES—Sometimes people can be bothered by personal difficulties that get in the way of their yielding to the Lord. The kinds of difficulties which get in the way are numerous—psychological or emotional problems, difficulties in their family or living situation, financial problems, and so on. If we are aware of the difficulties, we can help people get through them—and we can help them open up to the Lord's healing and wisdom in the midst of the problem. These people need new freedom in imaging Jesus as a real part of daily life. Personal prayer, community and an awareness of inner healing as a long-range goal are important.

THEOLOGICAL AND SPIRITUAL DILEMMAS—People will often admit that holiness, charisms, moral changes or going to church are great for some people, but they do not want it personally. A participant may balk at the idea that God would want us to pray or would want to be involved in daily life. Another may have an undeveloped understanding of God. Some dwell in relativism (one belief is as good as another) or an overemphasis on personal independence. In such cases people are experiencing limits and we need to help them see the fullness of God's power, love and message. God wants them to experience the Holy Spirit, and the strength to dream God's dreams for us. There is sometimes a moral dilemma underneath some of this kind of thinking.

RELIGIOUS EXPERIENCE SEEKING—From time to time we encounter people who look upon baptism in the Holy Spirit as a "religious experience" which is good to have. They are keenly aware of emotional needs, but are weak in facing moral, intellectual, ecclesial and socio-political needs for conversion. It is helpful to point out that baptism in the Spirit empowers us for a life of service. Charisms and spiritual gifts are given to direct us toward the needs of the Church and the world around us.

LACK OF WILLINGNESS—People are sometimes willing to go part way in following Jesus through the power of the Holy Spirit, but not all the way, or at least not yet. They get frozen in one spot for a time. This is connected to issues of surrender. Many can see the value of the fruits and gifts of the Spirit, like wisdom, joy and love, but reject charisms like discernment, tongues, healing and prophecy. We all need a real eagerness for what the Lord will do. On the other hand it is good to know that not everyone experiences conversion at the same pace. Some need little breaks in the journey, which are OK as long as they do not become permanent.

Part I (E) Community Building

A carpenter could make a beautiful door, the most beautiful door in the world, but it must fit properly in order to be an important part of the house. It might be too big, or too wide, or too thin. There might be any number of things wrong with it. There is no guarantee that an excellent door is going to be a good part of a house. For that, the eye of an architect (or "master builder") is needed. The door does not only have to be beautiful and well made. It has to fit into the house and make the house a better house. The carpenter has to build the door according to the specifications of the house.

The same thing is true of the Life in the Spirit Seminar, which can be a door into the Christian life. What the Lord wants is a wide variety of ways to bring people into the Church, real opportunities like the Life in the Spirit Seminar that evangelize people and help them actualize or integrate their initiation into the Body of Christ. God's people need to be built up and made strong. Just as a beautiful door would be useless to a house if it could not be fit into the house, so the Life in the Spirit Seminar may turn out to be of little value if they do not fit into what God is building in a particular place, strengthening the Church in that area.

The Life in the Spirit Seminar is designed to be an introduction to a renewed life in the Spirit that is communal as well as individual. Scripture uses many images for the importance of our connections to one another: the parts of a body, brothers and sisters, being in the same boat, and clinging to the vine together. Experience shows that if a person does not make new connections with a faith community, the Life in the Spirit Seminar alone will not make a major difference in that person's life. The new life God has given will fade away. The Life in the Spirit Seminars all by themselves are not effective in the long run. More is needed as follow-up, either ongoing small faith communities, making contact with large renewal groups and movements, or strengthened liturgical participation in the Church.

Think of the Life in the Spirit Seminar as just one door into the life of a faith community. The sessions are designed as an evangelistic formation tool that helps people enter the life of a community, but are offered in the context of other opportunities for growth, worship and formation. Team members should know how the seminar fits into the overall picture of what is offered. We do not want to create a revolving door that brings people in and then out with no regard for what is further down the road, or down the hall in the house. A community may want to consider offering additional courses such as *Growth in the Spirit* by Ron Ryan (available through Charismatic Renewal Services in South Bend) or *Bringing Christ to My Everyday World* by John Boucher (Chariscenter USA).

CONTEXT OF THE PRAYER COMMUNITY

There are many types of groups who make use of the Life in the Spirit Seminars. Some of them are small prayer groups who offer a seminar from time to time when there are enough people who want one. Usually such seminars have only three or four people in them and it is an easy matter for these few people to become a regular part of the prayer community; but it is also important to expose people to regional resources beyond the small group in this kind of situation. Some of the groups who use the seminars are large communities or renewal centers that serve many people over a wide geographical area. For these groups, integrating people into local communities can be a complex task, and is most effective if sponsors are used and these sponsors know a variety of different resources. There are, of course, many other settings for the seminar. They can be offered as a part of an evangelistic Lenten program, as part of the preparation for adult candidates for sacraments, as follow-up for a healing Mass, and as a part of a ministry group's training. The issue of what happens to people after a seminar in these situations is a very important part of the decision to offer one in the first place. Connections and further opportunities for growth must be offered that are specific and explicit.

There are, however, a number of concerns that every group has to attend to, no matter how large, small or varied. The first is attracting a broad range of people to the seminar. What we want in the seminars are people who need to hear the Gospel message and are ready to turn to the Lord in a deeper way. We also want to kindle faith in those for whom Baptism, Confirmation, or First Eucharist was a matter of routine or convenience. God has so much more to offer. Often when people hear a lay person witness to a lively faith in a real Jesus, they become seriously interested. Ordinarily we do not seek out the skeptical, the merely curious, or the person who is not open to entering into or deepening a committed relationship with Christ. But God will draw people and we must not be alarmed by their spiritual state, but confident in God's love.

Part of the way we evangelize people is announcing and publicizing the seminar with simple clarity. When we announce them, we give people an idea of what to expect. The way we announce the seminar helps them decide whether they want to begin. If we want people who are interested in a change in their personal relationship with the Lord, we should say that. If we want people who are considering baptism in the Spirit, we should say that. If we want people who wonder why they should come to church, we should say that. We should give relevant concrete details: how many weeks it will be, when the sessions will be held, how long the sessions are. We can give a sneak preview by using a personal witness as part of the invitation and we can offer leaflets that explain life in the Spirit, in conjunction with an announcement or invitation. In large group settings, we can also employ greeters with clipboards who will answer questions and take the names of those who are interested. A letter can also be sent as a reminder of when the seminar actually begins. Another part of reaching out to people is educating the prayer group or community in evangelization. Most people come in response to another person's invitation and encouragement. If we find that the people who are coming to begin the seminar are confused about what happens then we need to explain the seminar to the others in the group. The more the community as a whole understands evangelization and how to invite people in their daily lives, the more likely it is that people will come.

Sometimes when a problem exists with the people who come, it stems from the way people have been invited. When people are pressured to come, often they are not open to the Lord. Or when people are encouraged to begin without being told what they are getting into, they may be unprepared to take part. The prayer group or community may need an education in how to invite and encourage others. An understanding of Catholic evangelization is essential.

ABOUT SPONSORS AND MENTORS

In larger communities, the work of caring for people can be divided between Life in the Spirit Seminar team members and "sponsors" that are not necessarily on the team. "Sponsors" are a group of people who take on the responsibility of helping people who come to the Life in the Spirit Seminar to be integrated into the life of the community. They contact the new person after the second week and begin to invite them to places at which they can make contact with the life of the community or prayer groups (smaller prayer groups, parties, liturgies or special services, places at which community members gather). They will often make an effort to introduce them to other people in the community as well. A main concern is to see that participants experience what Christian life means on a daily basis and to see that they feel accepted. If sponsors are not usually a part of the team then they do need some kind of training and constant updates as to what the faith community is offering before, during, and after the seminar is offered.

Each week the sponsor will try to talk to each person that he or she is responsible for, but not necessarily for a long period of time. The sponsor takes the responsibility to see that the person does not get lost and does not lack the help each one needs until he or she is a part of the faith community. Of course, people will come from many different levels of involvement to begin with. It is especially important that the sponsor keep in contact with the person for a few months after the seminar is over so that the person can make the transition from the seminar to other community gatherings without becoming disconnected.

EVANGELISTS AND SPONSORS—
LINKS TO THE COMMUNITY

In the fifteenth chapter of Romans, Paul says to the Christians at Rome: "Accept one another, then, for the glory of God, as Christ has accepted you." (Rm. 15:7) Paul was actually speaking about the attitude that all Christians should maintain towards one another in their communities, but this model is most appropriate for those working in the area of initiating others into the Christian life and into the life of the local faith community. Jesus also depicted the warmth and joy that there is in heaven when someone turns to God. We need the attitude prevalent in the parables of the lost sheep, the lost coin, and the prodigal son in Luke 15. We ought to welcome new brothers and sisters into our lives with the same kind of eagerness and love that Christ has for them.

Evangelization is something that we are learning about as a Church. Many Christians are trying to find more effective ways to proclaim the Good News of Jesus Christ. Yet often an essential element of evangelization is neglected—welcoming a person who becomes interested in the Lord. Many fail to continue in the Christian life because they can not find a home among believers in the local faith community. Few of these people can persevere on their own. So we must take both evangelization and community building very seriously, as two sides of the same coin. Another way of thinking about the whole process is as a circle in which we invite people to conversion, integrate them into the community, then they in turn befriend more people who are invited to meet Jesus and experience conversion. And so the body of Christ grows. The Life in the Spirit Seminar has an evangelistic purpose, but they are primarily designed for instruction and faith formation. In the seminar, people can make contact with a Christian community, learn about the life in God's Spirit, and surrender to a fuller relationship with God. The Life in the Spirit Seminar must be part of an ongoing process of sponsorship, through which we befriend people. Then the community becomes their context for a new and growing faith.

Evangelizing and sponsoring people means welcoming them into our communal life and helping them become a part of it. It is a type of pastoral activity and an act of hospitality in the broadest and deepest sense. It is a ministry that is for every believer. Neighborhoods and extended families offered this support on a real spiritual level in the past. Today sponsoring or mentoring newly initiated Christians must involve a conscious effort. It can happen within a small faith-sharing group where people have learned to love others the way Christ loves them. Such Christians will naturally keep in contact with new people and include them in their life. One group that often befriends people is the team for the Life in the Spirit Seminar. They are in personal contact with new people from the very beginning. In a small prayer group, those who work on the seminar will often become sponsors and mentors in their work as team members. But this vision must also develop in the parish community as well.

The growth of a community or prayer group will usually create a need for a more deliberate means of befriending people. When a group of Christians gets to be larger than thirty or forty people, newcomers are no longer so noticeable, and so they no longer get welcomed. Some sort of pastoral concern is needed. Also when the Life in the Spirit Seminar is being given for people who live over a wide geographical area or in a prayer group or community that is large enough to have smaller sub-groups, there is a particular need to have a better way to befriend new people. The sessions themselves can be presented centrally without losing any effectiveness, but each new person needs to be connected with a sub-group of the community in the person's geographic area. The person who sponsors participants in the seminar must be familiar with the part of the community that the new person will be connected with. The sponsor is the link between the central seminar and the sub-grouping or local situation.

Sponsoring and evangelization only work when there is something to welcome new people into. It makes no sense to have a team of sponsors if there is not a group of people who have some kind of real commitment to living the life of the Spirit with one another. The purpose of sponsoring is to connect those who are newly interested in living that life together and who can help.

Every group also needs to pay attention to knitting the people who come to the seminar into the life of the community. The transition has to be made from the seminar to becoming part of the prayer group or community. Many will not continue past the Life in the Spirit Seminar without help. In order to go on, they have to be encouraged in the seminar. The last two weeks of the seminar should make this a special concern. They also have to be drawn into the life of the community. Many times, the difference between someone staying or going is simply some personal contact with others in the prayer group or community. When bonds are formed and love grows, a person is much more likely to go on. People need to get to know others outside of a formal meeting time. In smaller groups, the team members can take this responsibility.

Finally, every group has to attend to what is needed after the seminar. The seminar is not enough. People need much more help than the seminar gives. Different groups can do different things. Large, mature communities can provide further courses and helps of various kinds. Smaller groups or newer groups often can do little more than offer love and encouragement. We can only do what the Lord assigns to us, but nonetheless we need to make growth beyond the seminar our prayerful concern.

Part I (F) Time-line for Preparations

The size and abilities of the various kinds of groups that decide to offer Life in the Spirit Seminars varies a great deal, as does the size and background of the team itself. For this reason we are suggesting a time-line that assumes there is no on-going team. If you have a small team and are unaccustomed to planning ahead, choose a few important tasks to add to what you already do. Add more later.

SIX MONTHS PRIOR TO SEMINAR PREPARATION MEETING: A decision is made by the sponsoring group to offer a Life in the Spirit Seminar (at least four months before the proposed starting date). A part of this decision is compiling a list of possible team members to invite to long-range planning meetings and to any training sessions. A seminar leader is chosen who will take responsibility for further meetings. Decisions about team training should be made—whether it will occur as part of meetings or in a workshop setting. Another element would be drawing up a plan for an evangelistic event or a procedure for inviting participants. This plan would also be offered to the team later. See the "Explanation and sign-up Session" of the manual. Arrangements are made for the use of facilities. A schedule for the seminar is decided. An available site is chosen.

THREE TO FOUR MONTHS BEFORE SEMINAR STARTING DATE: First team meeting is to assign different responsibilities, set up publicity or invitation process, and decide on study materials to be given or sold. Order materials.

TWO MONTHS BEFORE STARTING: Research and decide on follow-up options for participants and assign someone to prepare invitational materials for participants. Decide about a possible reunion after the seminar.

SIX WEEKS BEFORE STARTING: Study the initiation process, invite sponsors. Publicity begins for the seminar. Appoint someone to handle books.

FOUR WEEKS BEFORE STARTING: Discuss purpose and skills involved in faith-sharing groups, practice handling needs in a sharing group

TWO WEEKS BEFORE STARTING: Evaluate preparations, assign partners to review talks and witnesses

ONE WEEK BEFORE STARTING: Go over sign-up lists and decide on groups and sponsors. Lists of participants are given so that welcoming phone calls can be made.

DURING THE SEMINAR: Team meets briefly after each session, or on a different night, in preparation for the next week

TWO WEEKS AFTER THE SEMINAR: Evaluation meeting (See evaluation section)

PART II: THE SEMINAR SESSIONS

Part II (A)
Explanation and Sign-Up Session

GOAL

To give a brief, clear explanation of the Christian message and God's invitation to a real and vital spiritual life. To present the Life in the Spirit Seminar as an opportunity to experience the fire of the Spirit who enlivens our relationship with Jesus. To provide sign-up for the seminar.

The 1979 version of the Life in the Spirit Seminar offered an approach to explanation sessions that is useful for larger prayer communities with regular weekly meetings. In such cases, prayer groups found explanation sessions before or after their meetings to be very valuable. Weekly explanation sessions provide an introduction to "what's going on around here" and allow visitors to ask questions. It is a way to evangelize and draw people to the Lord. This approach is also helpful for large regional gatherings. The explanation session can also be done in a variety of ways for other kinds of groups and the ministry needs they are responding to. For many smaller groups such a session can be offered on a seasonal basis.

Several regions in the country are also sponsoring large evangelistic events that include a proclamation of the Gospel and an invitation to a more vital life in the Spirit through the seminar. This can be done as a part of a regional conference. It has also been done in several states as a part of an evangelistic approach to healing masses, and even to Ash Wednesday services and Lenten formation. (See both the *Healing Mass Project*, and *From Ashes to Fire: A Process for Lenten, Eastertime and Pentecost Evangelization* which are produced by CRS of LI., PO Box 2151, Brentwood, NY 11717.)

THE TEAM MEETINGS

Sometimes a separate team works on the explanation and sign-up sessions, especially if they are done on a regular basis, or if a large evangelistic event will be used for this purpose. There should be a team meeting two months before the beginning of their period of service, another at the end, and evaluation sessions during the time they are working together.

TEAM MEETING (BUSINESS PORTION)

1. Discuss the explanation session
   • go over the talk and the format
   • go over the team member's sharing
   • share about the type of people who might come and approaches the team should take

2. Pray for the session and people who will come

THE EXPLANATION AND SIGN-UP SESSION

I. Greeting and introduction—of speaker, the session, and the group

II. Presentation
   A. God loves us and has created each of us for a full, happy life in union with the Father, Son and Spirit. This love is evident in many ways throughout the history of the world but especially in the coming of Jesus.
   B. Our efforts to find happiness and our own inner longings often fail to satisfy us. We often lose sight of the vision of eternal life and reject God through sin, but God is our happiness and the source of all goodness and life.

    C. Jesus Christ has come to give us the power to live this life. Through him we can know God's love and share in God's life with others.

    D. Faith in God means accepting Jesus Christ into every part of our lives as Lord and Redeemer. Faith in God also means baptism in the Spirit of Jesus, and an ongoing immersion in the life of God.

III. Why come to the Life in the Spirit Seminar
    A. Learn about Pentecost and what it can mean for us
    B. Discover a renewal that millions of Catholics have experienced

IV. A brief invitation that mentions time, place, team
    A. One or two witnesses from people who have attended
    B. Question and answer period—followed by concluding prayer

V. Actual sign-up—several people are available with lists (and they can also answer questions)

COMMENT ON THE DYNAMICS

The explanation session is designed to be short (20 minute talk, two 5 minute witnesses, 15 minutes of questions and answers, 10 minutes for sign-up). The expanded outline below provides some choices in what is offered.

The question and answer period in a very large group can be handled in several different ways. The first involves letting people generate questions and concerns with a partner first, then voicing them in the large group. A second approach involves dividing people into small groups of seven or eight with a team member in each group to handle questions. If the speaker is alone or if the group is small the questions can be handled accordingly. The team members should expect to get some rough questions: (Will people who never heard of Jesus be condemned to hell? How come the pope said...?, etc.) They should not try to answer questions that they can not answer. Insofar as possible they should try to keep the discussion centered on the basic Christian message.

EXPANDED OUTLINE OF THE PRESENTATION

I. Introduction

Today we have gathered in the presence of God and sought to experience the reality of Jesus and his transforming Spirit. (State any other goals of session here.) We have come together to hear the message of the Gospel and to the listen for the way these words of life echo in our hearts, minds and souls. Let us take a closer look at the message and the invitation.

II. Presentation

In order to understand what we are experiencing it is necessary to understand the basic message of the Gospel (the kerygma). An example of this message can be seen in Peter's address to the crowds on Pentecost. This message is also the skeleton of both the Apostles' Creed and the Nicene Creed that we proclaim together every time we celebrate a Eucharist together. (Statements from the Creeds are in bold print.)

A. God loves us and has created each of us for a full, happy life in union with the Father, Son and Spirit. This love is evident in many ways throughout the history of the world but especially in the coming of Jesus. This is why, as part of our creed, we say: **I believe in God, the Father almighty, creator of heaven and earth.**

B. Our efforts to find happiness and our own inner longings often fail to satisfy us. We have lost sight of the vision of eternal life with God as our central goal.

Humanity has fallen short. We often find ourselves separated from God, and prone to sin. Each of us is in need of God's help in order to experience God's love and share the life of the Trinity with others. "Everyone has sinned and is far away from God's saving presence." (Rm. 3:23) Sin involves indifference and rebellion toward God. Humanity's separation from God also results in one person's separation from another. We need a spiritual change that only God can produce.

"Because those people refuse to keep in mind the true knowledge about God . . . they do the things that they should not do. They are filled with all kinds of wickedness, evil, greed, and vice." (Rm. 1:28-29)

This is why we say:

We believe in one Lord, Jesus Christ, the only Son of God.... Through him all things were made. For us men and for our salvation he came down from heaven.

"I have come in order that you might have life—life in all its fullness." (Jn. 10:10)

C. Jesus Christ has come to give us the power to live this life. Through him we can know God's love and share in God's life with others.

"For God loved the world so much that he gave his only son, so that everyone who believes in him may not die but have eternal life." (Jn. 3:16) In Jesus, God became human and entered the world to overcome the separation between God and humanity. Through his life, death, and resurrection Jesus Christ has made it possible for us to experience this abundant life.

"I am the way, the truth, and the life: no one goes to the Father except by me." (Jn. 14:6)

D. Faith in God means accepting Jesus Christ into every part of our lives as Lord and Redeemer. Faith in God means an ongoing immersion into the life of God.

1. Accepting Christ into your life is more than an intellectual belief that Jesus was God and died for us. It is more than just doing good works and following his (moral) teaching. It means entering into a personal relationship with Jesus and growing in his love as we surrender our lives, especially through and with his Body, the Church.

   Each one of us must look at what we hold dear at the core of our being, the center of life—the driver's seat. Each of us must ask, "What is my life centered around? What is my most burning desire?" Whatever I hold in my heart is what controls my life. Sometimes it is another person, an interest or a personal goal. Christ may be one of many interests, or not even a factor in our lives.

   To accept Jesus means allowing him to take the center of our beings and fill it with love. It involves surrendering our lives to him, and embracing God's life that was freely given to us at Baptism. It means knowing God personally.

   "Some, however, did receive him and believed in him; so he gave them the right to become God's children." (Jn. 1:12)

2. Faith also involves imitating Jesus who was immersed in the Spirit during his baptism and promises the gift of the Holy Spirit to his followers.

   In all four Gospels John the Baptist says of Jesus, "He will baptize you with the Holy Spirit." (Mk. 1:8, Luke 3:16, Matthew 3:11)

   Jesus promised the Holy Spirit to his followers (Jn. 16:12-13, Jn. 14:16-17).

   Just before his Ascension he said, "John baptized with water, but in a few days you will be baptized with the Holy Spirit." (Acts 1:5) He promised an immersion that would be ongoing, not a one-time event.

This is why, as part of our creed, we say:
I believe in the Holy Spirit, the holy catholic Church, the communion of saints....

III. Why join a Life in the Spirit Seminar

[Points A, B, and C are optional, as time permits, and can be covered by giving people an introductory booklet, as well as in witnesses.]

A. Learn about the power and presence of the Spirit in the early Church
   1. Pentecost
      - the promise fulfilled (Acts 2:4)
      - the difference: boldness, power, unity, love, and effective
      - preaching of the gospel, conversions
      - manifestations of the Spirit: wisdom, zeal, prophecy, tongues,
      - inspired praise
   2. Pentecost happens several times in Acts. One could mention any of the following: Philip in Samaria (Acts 9), Paul and Ananias (Acts 9), Peter and Cornelius (Acts 10), Paul at Ephesus (Acts 19); or from St. Paul: Gal. 3:1-5, or 1 Thes. 1:2-10.
   3. Studies of the first several centuries of the Church reveal that a real experiential baptism in the Spirit (a personal Pentecost) was part of the normal process of being initiated into the Church. The imparting of charisms belonged in the catechumenate and in the celebration of the Sacraments of Initiation.

B. Discover a renewed life in the Spirit, the guiding force to our faith in Jesus.
   1. Today, in the Catholic Church there is growing

spiritual renewal. There seems to be an answer to the prayer which Pope John XXIII asked Catholics to pray during the Second Vatican Council (which occurred in the 1960s): "Renew in our day, O Lord, your wonders as by a new Pentecost."

2. Millions of Catholics have come to a release or a renewal in their experience of the power of the Spirit. A common result is new experiences of the reality of God. In 1975 Pope Paul VI greeted an international conference of the charismatic renewal with these words: "The Church and the world need more than ever that 'the miracle of Pentecost should continue in history.'"

   - the Spirit makes Scripture alive and gives a desire to tell others about Christ
   - desire for Christian community and growth through faith sharing
   - the Spirit gives charisms or "gifts" of the Spirit (tongues—a gift of prayer, prophecy or sensing a message inspired by the Holy Spirit, healing, discernment, almsgiving, hospitality and others too numerous to mention)
   - growth in the fruits of the Spirit (love, joy, peace, patience, kindness, goodness, faithfulness, gentleness and self-control—Gal. 5:22); the Holy Spirit begins to produce changes in character and attitudes so that we are able to act as Christ did.

C. The life in the Spirit is given in the Sacraments of Initiation (Baptism, Confirmation and Eucharist) and is for everyone. God will reactivate this gift of life.

[Abbreviated version resumes here]

The Life in the Spirit Seminar provides a way to learn more about life in the Spirit and baptism in the Spirit. It offers a vision of an ongoing immersion into the life, the promises, the power and the love of God.

(Describe the Seminar briefly and indicate when the next one starts.)

COMMENTS ON THE PRESENTATION

The speaker does not need to add much to this expanded outline. The most important addition he or she should make is **his or her own personal witness**, which should be given while describing the kind of differences the Holy Spirit makes in the life of a Christian. In fact, the whole last section could be given as a personal testimony.

In giving personal testimony, the speaker should describe the kind of life he or she led before recognizing Christ as Lord and the release of the Spirit. The speaker should share how he or she came to accept Jesus and experience new life in the Spirit. Then describe the kind of changes since then. Do not speak in generalities. When possible, the speakers should tell their stories of turning to the Lord and should add incidents that illustrate the points. The testimony should be short and simple.

Much of the power of the talk given in the explanation comes from its directness and simplicity. The speaker does not have to elaborate a great deal. The message speaks for itself in a powerful way. The scriptural stories and testimony will make the last sections of the talk effective.

Two or three team members should give the individual witnesses. It is good to have a variety of sharings: a younger person and an older person, a person who was not a practicing Catholic before he or she took the seminar, and a person who was already a practicing Catholic, but experienced a new release of the Spirit during the seminar.

The leader should plan a rotating schedule for the individual sharings if the team is larger that three people. Each one should be open to adjusting that schedule according to the type of people who come to the sign-up session. (If there were a large number of college students, for instance, a sharing from a college student would help.)

THE SIGN-UP SESSION
(ONLY WHEN DONE SEPARATELY)

COMMENTS ON THE DYNAMICS

The sign-up session should be relatively brief, not much more than half an hour altogether. The tone should be welcoming—warm, open, and friendly. The normal time to hold the session would be after a large gathering of the community or after an explanation of the renewal and the seminar. Should the gathering go later than usual, the session can be briefer.

The team members should be at the sign-up session room immediately after the end of the gathering. They should introduce themselves to the people who have come to sign up and talk with them informally. They should also be available to talk with people at the end of the session. It is a good idea to have refreshments available and to hold the session in a room that is inviting and comfortable.

EXPANDED OUTLINE OF THE PRESENTATION

A. Short description of the seminar
  1. Details like time and place: It lasts for seven weeks. We will meet for about two hours every _____ evening at ____ p.m. During the first four weeks we hear about the promises of Christ and the way we can respond to them, how we can live out our baptism in the Spirit. The fifth week involves prayer for the release of the Spirit of Jesus. The last two weeks teach us about growing in the life of the Spirit.
  2. The seminar is an opportunity to respond to God's message and love.
  3. Individual sharing:
     - share what made you decide to attend the seminar.

- share what happened to you during the seminar (how you came to know Christ and the Spirit; concrete changes you experienced during that time, e.g. experiencing God's presence, peace, joy, Scripture coming alive, and new ability to pray and praise God).

- share what has happened to you since the seminar (being drawn into Christian community or prayer group, being set free from obstacles, seeing the power of God at work in your life, personal relationships being improved, guidance, teaching).

SIGN-UP PROCEDURES

It is advisable to have one person in the parish, community or prayer group be responsible for assigning people to the seminar, even if several people are needed to compile lists or do data entry. It is also wise to send a letter, reminding people who have signed up, even if they have been told verbally, when the seminar begins. If groups are formed well enough in advance, the facilitator could also call people and welcome them.

HELPFUL RESOURCES FOR EXPLANATION SESSIONS

The desire to bring others to Jesus is at the heart of explaining the Gospel message and the value of the Life in the Spirit Seminar. **Team members** can learn more about Catholic evangelization by reading *Share the Good News* by Rev. John Bertolucci (St. Paul Books and Media 1993), *News that is Good: Evangelization for Catholics* by Rev. Robert J. Hater (Ave Maria Press, 1990) or **** *Go and Make Disciples: A National Plan and Strategy for Catholic Evangelization in the United States* (United States Catholic Conference, 1993). A study guide for this last document was written by Sue Blum and is available through the National Council of Catholic

Evangelization at 1-800-786- NCCE. We would also recommend **** *Toward a New Pentecost For a New Evangelization* (Malines Document I, Liturgical Press, 1993) edited by Rev. Kilian McDonnell, O.S.B. It divides material about the charismatic renewal into short sections that are good for group study and for answers to questions. For more resources in evangelization visit Therese Boucher's website www.christkey.com.

Participants can be given a copy of the **booklet**—*An Introduction to the Catholic Charismatic Renewal* by John and Therese Boucher (Servant Publications, 1994). It provides a brief description of the charismatic movement. They might also purchase books like **** *Still Riding the Wind* by Rev. George Montague, S.M. or *As By a New Pentecost: The Dramatic Beginnings of the Catholic Charismatic Renewal* by Patti Gallagher Mansfield.

Part II (B) Session 1: God's Love

GOAL

The 1979 edition reminds us of what is at the heart of this session. During the first session we reach out to people and begin to get to know them. It is a session of hope and of promise. In it we speak to people in a simple way about what God is offering. We share about God's love, about how God reaches out to us and offers us a personal relationship with him. God loves us in a very real and vital fashion, leading us deeper and deeper into an ongoing life of holiness.

"For God loved the world so much that he gave his only Son, so that everyone who believes in him may not die but have eternal life." (John 3:16) A loving Father offers us new life and sends the Spirit to dwell within us, so that we might be more closely united to Jesus than we are to anyone or anything else. God has befriended us and also offers new life through the action of the Holy Spirit.

The first session is an introduction, a session for encouragement. The presentation should be short (between 10 and 20 minutes) and should express confidence that God's presence and love will be evident in a significant way during the weeks of the seminar. The discussion time is for personal sharing, getting to know people, and discovering the variety of ways that God's love is and has been evident among us. We try to stir up in the participants a greater desire for God and a growing faith in the Lord. As Catholics we are like people on a treasure hunt, uncovering God's presence that has been a part of our whole lives, even if God seemed to be invisible, inattentive, or uncaring.

TEAM MEETING IMMEDIATELY BEFORE FIRST SESSION

1. Discuss the team members' roles in the seminar (See pages 18–35)

2. Preview the first session
   - understand the goal to be achieved
   - go over the format

3. Go over the purpose of faith-sharing groups and the questions

4. Discuss the role of the team member in the first session
   - be in the room before the people come in
   - be warm and friendly; introduce yourself
   - get to know the people and remember their names
   - stay around afterwards to talk and to get to know the people

5. Pray for the seminar and those who will come to them

THE FIRST SESSION

I. Greeting, introduction and prayer
   A. Registration—meet people as they arrive
   - Get names, addresses and phone numbers (unless this has been done during a previous introductory session).
   - If it is a small seminar, have people introduce themselves to each other.
   B. Leader's Introduction of the seminar
   The team leader introduces himself or herself.
   The Life in the Spirit Seminar is a means to a better life through Jesus Christ:
   - It lasts seven weeks in all
   - It is important to attend every session
   - Each session brings out part of the whole picture

(if someone can not make a session for some unavoidable reason, please tell me ahead of time and we will arrange a way for you to make it up)
- There will be time to listen to people share about their faith and the message of the Gospel, time for gathering in small groups, time for prayerful worship and an informal coffee break.
- Urge people to attend all the sessions, in order to experience real formation.
C. Prayer and praise

II. Presentation
A. God loves us and wants to be in a personal relationship with us. God is love and offers us the fullness of life and holiness.
B. During the Life in the Spirit Seminar we will look at God's invitation to enter into this love and to choose the saving presence of Jesus Christ, as well as the life of God's Holy Spirit.
C. God has begun this new life in us through the sacraments of Baptism, Confirmation and Eucharist. During the seminar we hope to rediscover this gift.

III. Witness by a team member about **the discovery of God's personal love**.

IV. The Faith-sharing groups
A. Leaders or facilitators for small group sharing are introduced and people are assigned to their groups. (We recommend earlier sign-ups and pre-arranged groups. Only walk-ins would be placed at this time.)
B. The leader invites people to introduce themselves to one another, and to share how they decided to come to the Life in the Spirit Seminar.
C. Then the leader offers a sharing question or two: What brought you to the seminar? How do people you know search for happiness and peace, or for God? What does it mean to have an intimate and personal

relationship with God? How do you feel when you approach God? Towards the end of the sharing time the facilitator may share a brief witness to God's personal, unconditional love. REMEMBER: If the group gets stuck on a question it is always appropriate to ask "What struck you during the talk we just heard?"

V. A. Closing prayer in the large group—Invite people to turn to the Lord in a few moments of prayer, singing a hymn, or through a meditative reading of one of the Scriptures in the talk.
   B. Announcements about next week—Distribute any pamphlets and daily reading booklets such as Finding New Life in the Spirit. Give instructions on the importance of using this booklet every day. It is also a good idea to give them copies of the commitment prayer in session 5 as a preview of what the seminar will touch upon. Encourage them to pray it every day.

COMMENTS ON THE DYNAMICS

We want to welcome people during this the first session, and make them feel at ease. We want to love them and be available in sensitive and caring ways. In the first session, we are dealing with people who may feel like outsiders in relation to the sponsoring prayer group, the parish, or the Church in general. We should speak to them in a way that will encourage them, and we should speak to them in ways that welcome them as brothers and sisters. As Paul say, "You are not foreigners or strangers any longer; you are now citizens together with God's people and members of the family of God." (Eph. 2:19)

The purpose of the first discussion is to foster personal sharing about people's relationships with God, and to help people feel comfortable talking about their faith. The sharing will also introduce people to one another. It will take the seminar out of a theoretical level on to a personal level. Finally, the sharing group facilitator can become a model for ways to talk about God. People need a safe and respectful place where God can be spoken about.

We should also be punctual and stick to our agreements about when the session ends. Then remind people of the time and place for the next session. The length of the session should be something that people can count on.

EXPANDED OUTLINE OF THE PRESENTATION

II. Presentation

    A. God loves us unconditionally and has created each of us for a full, happy life in union with the one God who is Father, Son and Spirit. We can see evidence of love in creation.

        1. The human heart is filled with all kinds of dreams, desires, hopes and plans. We search for health, happiness, and security. All of these desires point us toward something more, a bigger dream, a greater hope, and a sense of meaning and purpose in life.

        2. Our efforts to find happiness and our own inner longings often fail to satisfy us. We can easily lose sight of the vision of eternal life that God offers us. (cf. Is. 55:1-3) God says, "Come, listen and live."

    B. God wants the intimacy of a personal relationship with each of us. God acts. God speaks. God touches us and intervenes in our lives. God is love and offers us the fullness of life. Throughout history God has offered a covenant, a promise of love, that is both individual and communal. Each of us is invited to experience the vastness of God's love as a part of the "People of God."

- This is why as part our creed we say:
I believe in God, the Father almighty, creator of heaven and earth.

C. God has begun this new life in us through the sacraments of Baptism, Confirmation and Eucharist. God's love and presence is ours as life-long gift. The word "baptism" means to immerse or plunge. *The Catechism of the Catholic Church* also calls Baptism "the washing of regeneration and renewal by the Holy Spirit." (CCC # 1215) During the Life in the Spirit Seminar we will look at our response to God's gift of life and what this renewal in the Spirit means for us.

1. We were baptized in the name of the Trinity. We must look at what it means to be sustained by a Father's love, to choose the saving presence of Jesus—who is Lord and Christ—and to be immersed in the life of God's Holy Spirit, like a fish living in and through water.

2. The Life in the Spirit Seminar is an opportunity to explore and ratify our Baptismal Vows so that we can grow in our life in the Spirit. It helps us focus on living the Sign of the Cross and the creed as our response to God. Our on-going goal is to be mature disciples and followers of Jesus Christ. As Padre Pio said, "Go ahead! Courage! In the spiritual life he who does not go forward goes backward. It is the same with a (sail) boat that must always go forward. If it stands still the wind will blow it back."

   a. If you have been baptized but are a Catholic in name only, or if you are seriously considering the Sacraments of Initiation (Baptism, Confirmation and Eucharist), God will offer you a new beginning—a genuine relationship with Jesus, that has perhaps only been seen in brief glimpses over the years. Many people with only an elementary grasp of faith may "need to complete or modify their own initiation." (*General Directory for Catechesis*, No. 49) This means a radical acceptance of God, who has already loved us.

b. Those who have been trying to live the Christian life but do not seem to be able to sustain a life of faith will discover how to yield areas of their lives to God's Holy Spirit.

c. Catholics who have already experienced an ongoing, personal relationship with Christ, will have the chance to be (re)rooted in the message of the gospel and the promises of Pentecost.

CLOSING PRAYER

V. A. Closing Prayer in the large group—Let us turn to the Lord together
(Spontaneous prayer, singing a hymn, or a meditative reading of one of the Scriptures in the talk).

- Let us acknowledge God's love and come into God's presence. "Then you will call to me. You will come and pray to me, and I will answer you. You will seek me, and you will find me because you will seek me with all your heart." (Jer. 29:12-13)

- End with a familiar prayer like the Our Father. We might also invite people to make the sign of the cross on one another's foreheads, as is done during Baptism. and again when we were confirmed.

B. Announcements: about any pamphlets, prayers and daily reading booklets such as *Finding New Life in the Spirit*.

- Pray every day to the Lord. Start tonight.

- Meditate on God's Word (explain how to use booklets. Point out first day and week **AND/OR** give them copies of the commitment prayer in this manual.)

- Suggested readings (If no booklets are given, these can be offered, but be careful not to overwhelm people with "homework."
- Since many are unfamiliar with Scripture, these could be printed on a sheet, or added to the bottom of an outline for the talk.)
  Suggested readings: Ps. 139, Ez. 34:11-16, Rm. 8:28-39

COMMENTS ON THE PRESENTATION

Introduction: At the beginning we must emphasize the importance of attending all the sessions, since all the sessions taken together provide a real opportunity for spiritual formation. We need not fear discouraging people by stressing attendance. We are gently but firmly offering a process for conversion and growth that takes time. We are building relationships with God and with one another by forming a faith sharing community.

Sections A and B of the presentation can be done in the form of a brief personal testimony, or each point can be illustrated with a personal example. We want to assure people who have had bad or inadequate experiences with Christianity that there is always more; we want to offer a vision of a fuller life through knowing God. One of the best ways to communicate this vision is through witnessing, telling others how these very things happened in our own lives.

The speaker should keep in mind that if he or she is going to give the presentation in Session 3, that the two testimonies should be somewhat different. This first testimony should center on the reality of God's love and our confidence in God. It should emphasize the fact that we can actually know God on many different levels, and not just by hearsay. The second testimony will center more on the outpouring of the Spirit and all that comes through a vital relationship with the Holy Spirit.

Commentary in the 1979 edition about Section C raises

the possibility that some people in the seminar will be coming from negative experiences with the Church. Some may have had a strong emphasis on rigid rules and practices, or a parish life that stressed loving other people at the expense of developing a personal relationship with Jesus Christ, especially in prayer. Both forms of Christianity make God seem distant. There will also be people coming with an authentic faith. When we talk about misconceptions of Christianity, or levels of faith we must be careful not to condemn valid ways of living out our Catholicism. Our only purpose is to assure those who have had difficult past experiences that they will be able to explore the heart of our faith during the Life in the Spirit Seminar.

In the present edition the categories of belief are more closely based on the church's understanding of people who need "initiatory catechesis" (beginner's lessons in the basic Christian life). The goal of this session is to acknowledge the wide variety of backgrounds and responses. Explain that many responses are possible and normal during the seminar. Expect to see all sorts of wonders and conversions. Some people will experience big changes. For some, an unexpected dimension of the Christian life will be experienced. Others will see the Spirit at work in their lives today, and even retroactively in past events. Some who already know the Lord can develop a new sense of the charismatic dimensions of faith. Most will find instruction and inspiration to grow. This would also be a good place to mention preparation for Sacraments of Initiation that is available through the RCIA in most local parishes.

Section V: The final announcement helps participants come into God's presence and sets goals for daily prayer. This short exhortation to turn to the Lord is an invitation. In it we share advice on the importance of prayer, meditation, and reading. Telling the people in the seminar what they can do during the week to make it much easier for them to open up to the Lord. Acknowledge that it is hard to start a new habit. Be patient with yourself in answering this invitation from God.

HELPFUL RESOURCES

Some passages that might be used in this talk to support what the speaker is saying: Jn. 3:16, Jn. 1:12, Jn. 10:10b, Jn. 14:23, Rev. 3:20, Is. 45:18-19, Ez. 34:15-16, Ps. 145:18. A **primary reference book for team** members that applies to all the material in talks would be the **** *Catechism of the Catholic Church* (Liguouri Publications, 1994 or Doubleday, 1995). We also recommend *The One Year Guide to the Catechism of the Catholic Church* by Gerry Rauch (Servant, 1999). Additional insights for team members are outlined in *Born of The Spirit* by Ron Ryan (Western Washington Catholic Charismatic Renewal, 1988). It is also advisable to sell the same books that were recommended during the explanation session (ex. by Mansfield and Montague).

Part II (C) Session 2: Salvation

GOAL

To help people see the magnitude and importance of Christ, to help them understand the basic Gospel message (what Jesus does), and to help them answer the invitation to follow Jesus. "For God loved the world so much that he gave his only Son, so that everyone who believes in him may not die but have eternal life." (Jn. 3:16) The second session presents the Good News about Jesus who is Shepherd, Healer, Lord, and Redeemer. Jesus ushers us into God's kingdom that involves committing and recommitting ourselves to a way of life. As we follow Jesus there are real choices between good and evil, between holiness and sin. These choices make knowing Jesus as our redemption very concrete.

TEAM MEETING (BUSINESS) BEFORE THE SECOND SESSION

1. Review last week's session
   - discuss any problems that appeared and what to do about them
   - go over the list of people and consider what should be done for each one
   - work out the final faith-sharing groups

2. Preview the second session
   - understand the goal, the format and the talk

3. Discuss what the team member should do
   - the need to still be welcoming and to get to know people in the seminar
   - review the goals and progress of the sharing groups as well as the questions

4. Pray for the seminar and those in it

THE SECOND SESSION

I. Introductory greeting and a time of praise and worship

II. Presentation
   A. God sent Jesus, his Son, to give us new life. Jesus reveals the Father's love for us. Through his life, death and resurrection Jesus is Shepherd, Healer, Lord and Savior.
   B. Jesus invites us into a Kingdom, a new way of life, a gift of redemption. We are created in God's image, but fallen and tarnished. We are all affected by original sin. Jesus offers forgiveness and restoration for each of us and for the whole world.
   C. We need God and have a choice to make in order to live this new life. Each day we must answer the Scriptural question Jesus asked Peter, "Who do you say that I am?" (Mark 8:27) We can also look at Mary who is as an example of responding to God's love and invitation to accept Jesus.
   D. When we were baptized, no matter how long ago, vows were made as part of the sacrament. We (or our parents) promised to reject sin, to believe in God who is Father, Son and Holy Spirit and to embrace the Church. These vows are also a life-long commitment, a striving for intimacy with God.

III. Witness (given by a different person) to **discovering and knowing Jesus**

IV. The Faith-sharing group
   Sharing questions: What kind of a mental picture do you have of Jesus? Which of the Scriptural titles for Jesus are meaningful for you: (read them twice) Good Shepherd, Lord, King of Kings, Christ, Lamb of God, Son of Mary, Savior, Healer, Brother, Emmanuel, Word of God, Bread of life. Say something about your choice. What do your baptismal vows mean to you now?

V. Closing prayer (preceded by announcements)—We may
want to add that people come forward to bless themselves from a common bowl of holy water during a
song.

COMMENTS ON THE DYNAMICS

Much of what is true for the first session is also true
for the second session. From the point of view of the way
people feel, the second session is still introductory. The team
has to be welcoming. By the end of this session, each facilitator should know the people in the faith-sharing group,
and begin to have a grasp of each person's relationship with
the Lord. The witness of our faith usually strikes those who
do not realize that Jesus is alive.

EXPANDED OUTLINE OF THE PRESENTATION

II. Presentation
   A. God sent Jesus, his Son, to give us new life. Jesus
      reveals the Father's love for us. Through his life, death
      and resurrection Jesus is Shepherd, Healer, Lord and
      Savior.
      - Jesus is the Christ (the messiah, the one God sent)
        (Col. 1:13, Jn. 11:21-27, Mt. 16:13-17).
      - Jesus lived, died and rose from the dead to give us
        new life (Rm. 4:25, Col. 1:20, Tit. 3:3-7, Jn. 10:10b, Jn.
        4:14).

   B. Jesus invites us into a Kingdom, a new way of life, a
      gift of redemption. We are created in God's image, but
      fallen and tarnished. We are all affected by original
      sin. Jesus offers forgiveness and restoration for each of
      us and for the whole world.
      1. God made the world to be a place of peace and jus-
         tice and happiness, a place in which Jesus would

reign. "People will say, 'Let us go up the hill of the Lord, to the Temple of Israel's God. He will teach us what he wants us to do; we will walk in the paths he has chosen.'" (Is. 2:1-5)

2. The world is fallen from an original state of goodness (societal evils such as: war, poverty, riots, racial conflict, communication gap, exploitation). Individuals suffer from a fallen nature as well, through loneliness, isolation, depression, insecurities, meaninglessness and personal relationships characterized by fear, anger and mistrust. Jesus has come to address all these situations. Turn to Jesus.

3. Jesus has conquered the pervasive power of sin (Rm. 3:9, 23) and darkness (Col. 1:13). We are forgiven and can start over. Jesus gives us the strength to renounce the Devil who now has only limited power. (Rm. 8: 37-39) St. Ambrose said: "When we speak about wisdom, we are speaking of Christ. When we speak about virtue, we are speaking about Christ. When we speak about justice, we are speaking of Christ. When we speak about peace, we are speaking of Christ. When we speak about truth and life and redemption, we are speaking of Christ."

C. We need God and have a choice to make in order to find new life. We must answer the Scriptural question Jesus asked Peter, "Who do you say that I am?" Just like Peter, we must struggle with what this means. We are called to a life of discipleship as a way to live out our response. Every area of our personal and communal lives is meant to echo the truth that "Jesus Christ is Lord."

1. God has intervened to bring true peace, justice, and truth:
   - The spiritual realm is not an optional extra (Jn. 15:5c)
   - Only in God's kingdom are these things possible (Is. 2:1-5, Is. 45:22)

2. Jesus is Lord, bringing freedom and new life to those who accept him. (Mt. 28:18, Phil. 2:5-11) Jesus lives in each of us and in his Church and to bring life to those who are his followers (Eph. 2:17-22), for the sake of the world.

   - This is why in our creed we pray: **We believe in one Lord, Jesus Christ, the only Son of God.... Through him all things were made. For us men and for our salvation he came down from heaven.**

3. Mary is an example of the kind of surrender to God that brought Jesus into our midst. She can be an inspiration and guide for us.

4. We can ask ourselves what our own baptismal identity as followers of Jesus means to us now. Who do we say that Jesus is today?

D. When we were baptized, no matter how long ago vows were made as part of the sacrament. We (or our parents) promised to reject sin, to believe in God who is Father, Son and Holy Spirit and to embrace the Church. These vows are also a life-long commitment, a striving for intimacy with God.

   - An important question asked during Baptism is "What do you ask of God's Church?" Our answer is "Faith" in a person. At the heart of our answer is the Scriptural exclamation "Jesus Christ is Lord!" Jesus is my Lord (Phil. 2:11).

   - An ancient prayer summarizes the meaning that the name of Jesus holds for us. It is called the *Jesus Prayer* and goes—"Lord Jesus Christ, Son of God, have mercy on us sinners." Let's take some time to repeat it slowly together, then I will stop leading you and let you pray it silently to yourself for a few minutes.

   Next Week: We will consider what new life in Jesus looks like and what openness to the Spirit means. Remind them to use their booklets. If they are not being used, then give them three passages from the talk.

COMMENTS ON THE PRESENTATION

The purpose of this second talk is to help people realize who Jesus is and what he does. The speaker proclaims Jesus, and opens up spiritual realities. Speaking from a live faith and offering ways to speak about Jesus are a real service that is a part of the presentation. The 1979 version reminds us that "salvation" means "God saves us." When we talk about salvation, we talk about what God has done, is doing, and will do. Our redemption in Jesus is not limited to the ideas of the forgiveness of sins and admission into heaven. It also includes a personal knowledge of Christ. God is at work in Christ to bring us to a full life on earth, a life that involves peace and happiness, freedom from sin and Satan, healing, and spiritual power. God is at work to bring about the kingdom. The Father has sent Christ, who forms the Church to become a new people who live in God's Kingdom. Salvation is not just something for the future, it is now. Salvation is not just something that brings individual good, but also a whole new life for all of humanity.

Sections A and B of the talk state the good news of Jesus. God has become flesh in Jesus. Jesus is much more than we can imagine. A sense of awe and confidence is helpful and can foster new faith. An example is important to share here. We do not have to stress what is wrong. A short list will suffice. All we are saying is that there is something that is wrong with the world and with the human condition.

The section on sin, Satan, and darkness can be difficult. Our personal experiences of God's salvation will affect our ability to speak. If we have not yet experienced freedom from sin, or a call to radical changes based in the Gospel, we can not speak these words with faith and conviction. Ask God for help to see yourself enough to teach others. It is also important to present the cosmic view of salvation. Both place us in contact with spiritual realities. The speaker might also meditate on the two standards in the second week of the *Spiritual Exercises of St. Ignatius Loyola* (trans. by Louis Puhl from Loyola Press, 1994).

When we speak about Satan, it is important to keep a balanced view. On the one hand, some have encountered evil spirits, or at least have suspected such realities. Most of us have felt that what is wrong with the world is something that is bigger than we are, something, in fact, that is bigger than the sum total of what individuals have done wrong. We have felt that there was some force behind it. On the other hand, the Devil is a fallen and limited creature, not a god. We must always focus on the power and compassion of Jesus above all else.

In section C the participants will see both the gift and the choice that we have as Christians. Choosing Jesus and the life of the Spirit involves a lifetime of choices as we live out our faith in the world. Imagining ourselves in the story about Peter can be helpful. God gives us the strength to recognize and choose Jesus. (Mt. 16:17) To do so is a gift in and of itself.

Avoid the temptation to emphasize one part of what Jesus does. Some stress the incarnation and the fact that Jesus is one of us, avoiding the "foolishness of the cross." Paul said that "the work of the cross is folly to those who are perishing, but to us who are being saved it is the power of God." (1 Cor. 1:18) We can not make complete sense of Jesus without looking at the cross. Others stress that Jesus died on the cross as a sacrifice for our sins and unwittingly give the impression of a vengeful Father. They would say that it is Jesus' death and the shedding of his blood that saves us, forgetting the love and teaching that led up to the cross. We must keep both the incarnation and redemption in a kind of creative tension. Jesus' death was a culmination of the message and events of His whole life. Easter and Christmas go together in our hearts, minds and lives.

HELPFUL RESOURCES

For **participants**: **** *Titles of Jesus* by Rev. Michael Scanlon (Franciscan University Press, 1985) and Dove Pamphlet #211 The Jesus Prayer. Books to recommend: *Rekindle Your Love for Jesus* by Msgr. David Rosage (Servant, 1996), *Hungry for God* by Ralph Martin (Ignatius Press, 2000). For **team** members: *A Stranger at Your Door* by Rev. John Powell, S.J. (Servant Publications, 1996) and Sections 430 to 682 in the *Catechism of the Catholic Church.*

Part II (D) Session 3: New Life

GOAL

The third session centers on the promise of new life in Jesus. It helps participants realize the goodness of the gift being offered to them. An explanation of how Jesus lived in the Spirit is given. The Baptism of Jesus becomes our model for a vital relationship with the Lord and Giver of Life. A witness is given on the place of gifts, fruits and charisms of the Spirit in daily life.

"I have come in order that you might have life—life in all its fullness." (Jn. 10:10)

The third session centers on the new life that each person receives in Jesus. We explain what baptism in the Spirit means. Many people will turn to Christ in a new way, after hearing about the kind of personal changes that are possible through the indwelling and release of the Spirit.

The heart of this session is the personal witness. The bulk of the presentation is an explanation of how the speaker became open to baptism in the Spirit and a fuller life of discipleship, and how the Spirit has become a part of daily life. The personal testimony can make a powerful change in people's attitudes. It can also be the most effective teaching method. People can receive a lot of theory about what it means to be baptized in the Spirit, but when they can hear a story of what happened to someone when that person was baptized in the Spirit, they really begin to understand what the baptism in the Spirit is.

TEAM MEETING (BUSINESS) BEFORE THE THIRD SESSION

1. Review last week's session
   - discuss any problems that appeared and what to do about them
   - go over the list of people and consider what should be done for them

2. Preview the third session
   - understand the goal of the faith sharing groups and questions

3. Discuss the personal contact to be made after the fourth session
   - how to talk with each person about surrendering to baptism in the Spirit
   - what each person thinks baptism in the Spirit is; perceptions about charisms
   - what each person's attitude is toward repentance and sin
   - what he or she thinks will happen when each person is prayed with
   - the need to make an appointment with each person in the seminar this week for the week after the fourth session

4. Pray for the seminar and for those in it

THE THIRD SESSION

I. Greeting and opening praise and worship

II. Presentation
   A. The Father offers new life to all. Jesus came into the world to bring life. Jesus surrendered to the Spirit during his baptism in the Jordan, and gives the Holy Spirit, as the source of new life for his disciples.

B. Jesus is a model for accepting the Holy Spirit, who is our helper and our strength.
   When we accept life in the Spirit, we are given the power to follow Christ and serve as members of the Body of Christ. (Include personal testimony here.)
C. There is always more of God's life and Spirit. We are constantly invited to experience a new and more vital contact with God. We have been baptized both in water and in the Spirit. Baptism in the Spirit may be a new idea for some of us. It means an ongoing and ever deepening spiritual life. It means a lifetime of graces, fruits, gifts and charisms rooted in our sacramental Baptism and Confirmation. We will say more about this next week.
D. Tell participants that we will have an opportunity for individual prayer for the release of the Holy Spirit two weeks from now. Someone from your faith-sharing group will help you discern what this would mean for you now.

III. Witness about **surrender to the Spirit**

IV. The Faith-sharing group
A. Discussion starters: What do you think it was like to see Jesus baptized in the Jordan, and later to see him heal the blind and the deaf? What does it mean to have a personal relationship with the Holy Spirit? Do you need Breath, Fire, Wind, a Helper or an Advocate in your life? Why?
B. After the small group session make an appointment to meet with each person during the week after the next session.

V. Closing Prayer and announcements
   If you will be using the Commitment Prayer in Session 5, option 2, distribute copies of it and ask participants to begin praying it. If you will be using the "Commitment Prayer" on page 25 in *Finding New Life in*

the Spirit ask participants to begin praying it. Remind them to use their booklets. If they are not being used, then give them passages from the talk.

COMMENTS ON THE DYNAMICS

There is usually a change in people during the third session. Most people are affected by the talk. A more lively faith and a deeper desire to change are coming to birth in their hearts. The role of the team is to foster that new faith and new desire.

The **individual contact** after the fourth week and before praying for baptism in the Spirit is essential. We make the appointment this week to insure that the person will be available during the week prior to the fifth session. For most people, a week and a half is enough notice, but not for everyone. We tell them that we need to speak with them individually before praying for baptism in the Spirit. When the faith sharing leader and/or sponsor meets with each person several things can happen:

1) It allows for answers to questions people still have about baptism in the Spirit. Some people need to think things through in a more personal setting. There can be questions that the person did not feel free to ask in a larger group; or sometimes, even if questions have already been discussed, a person needs to be reassured. Some also need help to explore Scriptural images for the Spirit. (See CCC # 691–701.)

2) The meeting can also encourage people to pray with faith. Their natural fears and hesitations, and Satan, are at work to keep them from placing their trust in God. Contact with a team member can help the person realize that fears are natural and so are temptations.

3) The meeting can also be a time to talk in greater depth about the gifts and charisms of the Spirit that may seem unfamiliar, like praying in tongues or prophecy. We can provide some help in yielding to what the Spirit brings.

4) The meeting can be a time to discern what God is already doing in a person's life and what a person needs to pray for. Sometimes, prayer for baptism in the Spirit is not the place to start. The most common reasons are struggles with serious sin, a reluctance to renew or make a commitment to the Lord, or excessive fear of spiritual experiences. Sometimes when people wait for another week, the experience of seeing people receive the Spirit in new ways allays their fears. There are other needs that we can pray with a person for during the fifth week of the seminar. (Sometimes they will be baptized in the Spirit as they pray for other needs—like greater faith.)

5) It is good to have the commitment prayer or Baptismal Vows photocopied and given to the people in the seminar during the fourth week. (This can be found on page 134.) Some groups use this commitment prayer for all seven weeks of the seminar. During the personal contact, we can ask them what this prayer means to them, and if they are ready to make this commitment. Reviewing the prayer and vows with them will often reveal some difficulties.

Individual prayer and the laying on of hands: It is often possible and appropriate to pray over people for a growth in faith and a new commitment to the Lord before the fifth week. Whenever we discern that someone in our faith-sharing group needs help and feel that he or she will be open to the laying on of hands, we can pray with that person. Such prayer will often make a big difference. If we keep in mind that some participants are backtracking on their own initiation into the Christian life, then we can turn to the RCIA as a model. The process of becoming a Catholic includes frequent blessing prayers for greater strength and understanding.

It is also not uncommon for people to experience a renewed baptism in the Spirit on their own, without the laying on of hands. As people grow in faith, this happens. After the third session it becomes somewhat common. We should not be uneasy if it does happen. For most people, the fruits and charisms of the Spirit will appear as the fruit of a firmer commitment to Christ and a radical openness to the Holy Spirit.

EXPANDED OUTLINE OF THE PRESENTATION

II. Presentation
   A. The Father offers new life to all. Jesus came into the world to bring us God's life. Jesus surrendered to the Spirit during his baptism in the Jordan, and promises to unleash the source of new life, the Holy Spirit.
      1. The Father sent his son into the world to bring us new life:
         - Even though Jesus was conceived by the Holy Spirit he still sought baptism in the Jordan. "As soon as Jesus was baptized, he came up out of the water. Then heaven was opened to him, and he saw the Spirit of God coming down like a dove and lighting on him. Then a voice said from heaven, "This is my own dear Son, with whom I am pleased." (Mt. 3: 15-17)
      2. After Jesus rose from the dead and ascended to the Father, he sent the Holy Spirit to bring us new life (Acts 1:1-5).

   B. Jesus is a model for accepting the Holy Spirit. We can see evidence of the Spirit after his baptism—in his teaching, healing, ability to pray and the events in his life. We also have Mary and the saints who are model of surrender to the Spirit. St. Francis Cabrini said, "Oh! If only devotion to the Holy Spirit inflamed the world, then should we see the face of the earth renewed, and Faith and Charity would triumph!"
      1. The ministry of Jesus was characterized by the activity of the Spirit. In Luke, we find Jesus repeating the words of Isaiah with conviction. "The Spirit of the Lord is upon me, because he has chosen me to

bring good news to the poor. He has sent me to
proclaim liberty to captives and recovery of sight
to the blind." After Jesus proclaimed this reading
he said, "This passage of Scripture has come true
today, as you heard it being read." (Lk. 4:18, 20)

2. Choosing Jesus as Lord means choosing to live in
the Spirit of Jesus. When someone is immersed in
the Spirit and led like Jesus, that person becomes
changed (Acts 19:1-7), even if that change only
begins to occur many years after receiving the Sacraments of Initiation. We are called to ratify our
initiation into Christ and to live in the Spirit. We
need the Spirit who is Breath, Fire, Wind, Seal,
Advocate and Helper as we follow Jesus.

- This is why as part of the Nicene Creed we say:
**We believe in the Holy Spirit, the Lord, the
giver of life.**

C. There is always more of God's life through the
ongoing nature of the Sacraments of Initiation. We
are baptized in water and the Spirit. Baptism in the
Spirit means appropriating an ever-deepening life
in the Spirit. It means a lifetime of graces, fruits
and charisms. We are confirmed and strengthened
with oil and the Spirit.

(Here a personal witness is given with attention to
the points below. Ones that have not been a part of
your experience can be briefly mentioned.)

a. Through the Spirit God gives us a vital faith:
- ability to know God as a caring and always
loving Father
- seeing God's love and presence in the context of
day to day life
- the strength to choose Jesus as Lord, Lover and
center of life
- the desire to live as a disciple

b. God offers new ways to pray:
- prayer becomes more centered on God, less on
self

- prayer of praise and thanksgiving becomes possible and frequent
- discovery of the gifts and charisms involved in prayer, such as tongues, contemplation, prophecy, inspired images and songs, etc.

● c. The Scriptures, the liturgy, and the sacraments come to life.

 d. The fruit of the Spirit develops (love, joy, peace—see Gal. 5).

 e. Gifts and charisms are expected, given and used to serve within the Body of Christ (e.g. wisdom, healing, praying in tongues, discernment, almsgiving, hospitality, encouragement, administration, and teaching, among others—See 1 Cor. 12 and Romans 12 for a few examples)

- "Charisms are to be accepted with gratitude by the person who receives them and by all members of the Church as well. They are a wonderfully rich grace for the apostolic vitality and for the holiness of the entire Body of Christ, provided they are really genuine gifts of the Holy Spirit." (*Catechism of the Catholic Church*, no. 800)
- The desire to bring Jesus to others often gives direction to charisms.
- Explain tongues as prayer beyond words—See Rm. 8:26-27

D. We can pray for baptism in the Spirit and expect more and more of the Holy Spirit's presence in us. We will be praying with each of you in two weeks.

✳ 1. This is not our first reception of the Holy Spirit, but a release of his power that is already within us through Baptism, Confirmation and Eucharist.

 2. Different people see different changes as a result of praying for baptism in the Spirit. Some may be conscious of the Holy Spirit for the first time. Others who have known the Spirit's presence in their lives

can become aware of new changes that the Spirit brings about. God offers a deeper indwelling presence of the Spirit to everyone.

3. Sometimes our years of Christian living are seen in a new light. Many resources will be in better focus through a new awareness of the Spirit in us.

4. We come to see our initiation into Christ through Baptism, Confirmation and Eucharist as a dynamic force that sets us on journey toward spiritual maturity, helping us sustain daily communion and friendship with Christ, and enabling us to becoming a loving people.

Next Week: we will look at what it means to be a disciple of Christ, ever attentive to the Spirit and willing to serve the Body of Christ.

The Week After: we will pray for the release or deepening of baptism in the Spirit. We would ask you to meet with your sharing group facilitator (or sponsor) during the week before we pray for baptism in the Spirit (not this week but the next one). Please make an appointment tonight after the sharing group.

If you are interested in learning more about charisms, we would like to **recommend** Dove Leaflets: #43 The Gifts of the Spirit, #1 Baptism in the Spirit, and # 8 The Gift of Tongues. (You may want to give these to participants.)

COMMENTS ON THE PRESENTATION

The 1979 edition makes the following important points. There are many ways of explaining baptism in the Spirit. Some of them put a great emphasis on the conscious experience of the presence of the Holy Spirit. Catholics do not accept the view that conscious experience is the sole criterion of the presence of the Spirit. On the other hand, it would not be in accord with Catholic tradition to be indifferent to the real power and presence of the Spirit. Being baptized in the Spirit is a release of what has already been given in Baptism, Confirmation and Eucharist. Praying over people is not a sacramental action (at least, certainly not in the full theological sense of sacramental action). It is rather a way of helping people appropriate what has been given to them, in order to experience its full effect. Hence, baptism in the Spirit can be seen as a renewal and revitalization of the Sacraments of Initiation.

Terminology can be problematic. For example, if we use phrases like "baptism in the Spirit," "outpouring of the Spirit," or "anointing of the Spirit" we do not want to imply that sacramental baptism was only an immersion in water. (The Spirit has been present from that day, is now, and will be with the believer for all eternity.) What we are speaking of is not the initial gift of the Spirit, but a release of that gift, a breakthrough of sorts so that the presence and power of the Holy Spirit takes effect in deeper ways.

There is likewise a possible danger of confusion when New Testament texts on the reception of the Holy Spirit are used in the seminar. These texts describe situations where an initial gift of the Spirit coincided with what we know of as a sacramental encounter. (The earliest Christians were baptized as adults.) On the other hand, many Catholics who received sacraments as children can relate to Scriptural descriptions of baptism in the Spirit (cf. Acts 2:8, 10-11, 19). Many experience such manifestations of the Spirit as peace, joy, fervor, and charismatic gifts. A new way of believing is experienced.

While doctrinal clarity is important, the goal is to bring people to a more lively faith in the presence of the Holy Spirit in their lives. If people can see what is promised in the gift of the Spirit, they will examine their own lives for what is missing. Personal testimony is very important in this process. The speaker should explain what happens to normal people and thereby engender a greater hunger for the life of God's Spirit. The way we talk about baptism in the Spirit can make a big difference. It is not a question of getting **something** but a new life with **Someone**—with God. Living in the Spirit has to be the center of our concern, not just the experience of baptism in the Spirit.

The last twenty years of study and pastoral practice in the charismatic renewal add a further dimension to the discussion. For example, Fr. Francis Martin's book talks about baptism in the Spirit as answering a need in our time. "It is a grace by which people are enabled in ever more profound ways to interpret reality correctly, to understand the significance of the way God is acting in history, and to have confidence in him. It is a real grace for those who live in a culture where practically nothing is attributed to God." (*Baptism in the Holy Spirit*, page 38-39) There is also more work to be done in understanding how charisms function within public ritual.

Section A is meant to be a brief introduction. Its purpose is to recall the offer of new life that has been spoken about before in the seminar and to connect that offer of new life with the Holy Spirit. Briefly mention these points. Section B presents Jesus as a model of surrender to the Spirit. Followers of Jesus can also expect things to happens when they receive the gift of the Holy Spirit. Paul's experiences in Acts 19 are a good example. There are a number of passages in Scripture that can be used to introduce the section on what happens to a person when he or she is baptized in the Spirit. Acts 2, Acts 8, Acts 10-11, and Acts 19 all contain scenes in which people receive the Spirit. Whatever passages are used, the speaker should emphasize that real and noticeable change takes place in a person. The Holy Spirit is active. Mention that there are also changes that happen slowly, so we can not conclude that God is not working when dramatic things do not happen.

In Acts 19:1-7 Paul comes to Ephesus and meets a group of "disciples." He apparently thinks they are Christians, but senses that there is something missing. So he asks a question, "Did you receive the Holy Spirit when you believed?" For us, that would be a strange question to ask. Few of us would think of asking whether a person had received the Holy Spirit when we saw something missing in a person's life. And if we were asked such a question without an awareness of our baptism in the Spirit, many of us would not know how to answer. And yet Paul apparently expected Christians to know that they had received the Holy Spirit. The group of disciples in Acts 19 had only received the baptism of John the Baptist and had not been fully instructed as Christians. Paul completed their initiation into Christ, and when he laid hands on them the Holy Spirit came and something happened to them.

Section C talks about the release of the Spirit and is also meant to be the outline for a personal testimony. In it the speaker shares what has happened to him or her, sharing how items 1 to 5 happened. Section 5 is on charisms. Be specific about charisms in the personal testimony, and mention a great variety of gifts as well. Tongues should be explained as a gift of both individual and communal prayer. Tongues can also be used with interpretation to build up a group of Christians, but we do not want to go into that too much here.

In section D we want to say that life in the Spirit can be experienced in concrete ways. What happened to the early Christians, many of the saints and the speaker can happen to us. This life in the Spirit begins at Baptism, Confirmation and Eucharist, but takes time to develop, a lifetime. People in the seminar are at different points in their relationships with the Holy Spirit. Some have already experienced what the speaker is describing, and can expect more from the Spirit. Those who pray for a fresh release of the Spirit can expect a turning point that is just the beginning of a lifetime in the Spirit. We need an on-going desire for more of God that is the foundation of holiness. "Happy are those whose greatest desire is to do what God requires; God will satisfy them fully." (Mt. 5:6)

HELPFUL RESOURCES

Participants may enjoy praying with two booklets called **** *Devotions to the Holy Spirit* collected by Rev. Brian Moore, S.J. (Pauline Books and Media, 1976) or *Favorite Novenas to the Holy Spirit* by Rev. Father Lawrence Lvasik (Catholic Book Publishing, 1995). Even though you have recommended or given leaflets, you may want to mention books such as *Charisms—Gifts of God's Love* by Rev. Bob DeGrandis, SSJ (1997) and *Baptized in the Spirit and Spiritual Gifts* by Steve Clark (Servant). Audio tapes would include: *Pray Without Ceasing: Releasing the Spiritual Gift of Tongues* and *Prophecy Clinic* (both by John Boucher) produced by CRS of LI., Inc., PO Box 2151, Brentwood, NY 11717.

Team Members may want to study **** *Call to Holiness: Reflections on the Catholic Charismatic Renewal* by Most Rev. Paul Josef Cordes (Michael Glazier: The Liturgical Press, 1997) or *Refresh Your Life in the Spirit* by Babsie Bleasdell and Henry Liberstat (Servant, 1997).

Part II (E)
Session 4: Receiving God's Gift

GOAL

To help people embrace a life of conversion and to offer a greater appreciation of the life in the Spirit. Both are in and of themselves gifts from God. "Jesus answered, 'Those who drink the water that I will give them will never be thirsty again. The water that I will give them will become in them a spring which will provide them with life giving water and give them eternal life.'" (John 4:13-14)

The fourth session is one of preparation. The message of God's promise has been presented. Now is the time for those who are ready to go further. This is the "How to do it" week presenting a vision of discipleship. We should not attempt to do too much in this session. We do not have to stress complete dedication to Jesus and the demands of absolute discipleship, as much as a willingness to live a life of faith. We do not have to urge them to seek deep spiritual revelations. All we have to do is to help people take concrete steps that are a vital part of surrendering to baptism in the Spirit. Establishing or re-establishing a relationship with the Holy Spirit will allow God to work in their lives. God will lead in all these things.

TEAM MEETING (BUSINESS) BEFORE THE FOURTH SESSION

1. Review last week's session
   - discuss any problems that appeared and what to do about them
   - go over the list of people and consider what should be done for them

2. Preview the fourth session
   • understand the goal of the session and how things are
     going in the sharing groups
   • arrange to get more people to help with the fifth
     week, if needed

3. Discuss what is happening to people this week and how
   to help people understand and experience surrender to
   God and repentance
   • consider the different types of people and the special
     help they need
   • go over briefly the personal contact in the coming
     week and stress its importance

4. Pray for the seminar and the people in it

THE FOURTH SESSION

I. Introductory greeting and opening praise and worship

II. Presentation
   A. Living the new life God has begun in us through
      the Sacraments of Initiation (Baptism, Confirmation
      and Eucharist) involves falling in love with Jesus. The
      word "believe" comes from a German word meaning
      to fall in love. Just as Jesus abandoned himself to the
      Father and the Spirit with complete trust, so must we.
      Jesus gives us the gifts of faith, surrender, repentance
      and attentiveness to the Spirit.
   B. Following Jesus involves turning toward God and
      away from all those things which block our relation-
      ship with God. Jesus must be our only Lord. God gives
      us the Sacrament of Reconciliation to help us return
      to God.
   C. As we turn toward God and surrender our lives, then
      the Spirit fills us with new life. There is a new fire that
      burns within our hearts, and a river of life in our souls

which constantly refreshes and sustains us. Mary is an example of surrender to God.

- The Catholic understanding of receiving the Spirit is based in the events of Easter and Pentecost, as well as a dynamic understanding of the Sacraments of Initiation, especially Confirmation. In this way we receive the fullness of the Spirit along with the seven gifts of wisdom, understanding, counsel, fear of the Lord, fortitude, knowledge and piety. (Next week we will pray for a deeper experience of baptism in the Holy Spirit.)

III. Witness about **conversion and being a disciple**

IV. Faith-sharing group
   A. Sharing question: What importance do repentance, conversion or reconciliation have in your family? What mental picture do you have of the disciples on Pentecost? What do you expect to happen when we pray for baptism in the Spirit next week? How could charisms like healing, prophecy, wisdom, the gift of tongues help in daily life?
   B. The facilitator should help people share about the issue of conversion first, then baptism in the Spirit. Then the facilitator or a sponsor could share a short testimony to their own conversion to Jesus and baptism in the Spirit. The leader should include an example of the difficulties he or she may have had in falling in love with God.

V. A. Concluding Remarks (by the leader, after the sharing groups and closing prayer)
      Give a brief explanation of the format of session #5 and urge them to be faithful to the meeting with their sharing group leader or sponsor. Encourage them to talk with them about any difficulties. Remind them to use their booklets. If they are not being used, then give them three passages from the talk.
   B. Closing Prayer and Praise

COMMENTS ON THE DYNAMICS

From the beginning of the fourth session to the end of the fifth session, our main goal is to encourage people to respond with love and trust to God. We will do this by example, through personal contacts, in faith-sharing groups and by the way we pray with people. Of course, the message of repentance and conversion is demanding, but it should always be presented in the context of a loving God. Normally, people will be having problems with fear and doubt. We need to encourage the fainthearted and assure them of God's healing love and promises. They need personal assurance. They need to know that the problems they are experiencing are normal problems. They need to know that God's promises actually apply to them personally. They need to know that they can give up certain forms of wrongdoing and that the absence of that wrongdoing will not make them unhappy for the rest of their lives. They need to experience our loving concern and support.

When we are giving people advice about the Sacrament of Reconciliation, it would be good to recommend a priest who is familiar with the dynamics of the seminar and who would be willing to employ spontaneous prayer or prayer for inner healing as part of the sacrament.

When the faith sharing leader or sponsor shares how he or she turned to the Lord and has experienced baptism in the Spirit, he or she should focus on personal steps toward conversion and the life of the Spirit. The testimony should be restricted to the topic of the presentation.

(Additional help) This is the week to find extra people to help with prayer during the fifth session. Usually it is good for each facilitator to have help in praying with the people in his or her group, unless there are more than enough sponsors.

EXPANDED OUTLINE OF THE PRESENTATION

II. Presentation

A. Living the new life God has given us through the Sacraments of Initiation (Baptism, Confirmation and Eucharist) involves falling in love with Jesus.

1. God loves us (Session # 1); Jesus has come to bring redemption, healing and new life (Session #2); God gives us this new life through Baptism and the Holy Spirit (Session #3). We are called to a radical relationship with God, who will change and heal us, making us new.

2. The word "believe" comes from a German word meaning to fall in love. Just as Jesus abandoned himself to the Father and the Spirit with complete trust, so must we. Jesus gives us the gifts of faith, surrender, repentance and attentiveness to the Spirit. Faith means imitating Jesus who emptied himself out of love—Jesus "gave up all he had, and took the nature of a servant." (Phil. 2:5-11) Faith means responding to Jesus who has fallen in love with us first.

B. Through Baptism, Confirmation and Eucharist Jesus gives us faith and life. God's promises are real and stronger than any feelings, doubts, or obstacles we have experienced. This life is a gift that is given to us as we connect ourselves to the life, death and resurrection of Jesus.

1. Following Jesus involves turning toward God and away from all those things which block our relationship with God. Jesus must be our only Lord. This process of life-long conversion often involves the Sacrament of Reconciliation.

2. To follow Jesus means conversion, repentance and reconciliation. They all imply a change of direction, a reorientation of our lives, or at least a strict

attention to the road we are on and to our destination. Our baptismal vows include renouncing evil.
  a. choose Jesus as our destination, our heart's great-
     est passion, our Lord
     - turn toward God with every ounce of our beings,
       with all we do and own
     - choose God's life, not out of fear of punishment,
       or because of a reward
     - listen (obey) as children of a loving Father.
  b. turn away from all those things, which block our
     relationship with God; turning from sin involves
     repentance, which means:
     - honesty—admit that there are things that are
       wrong and need changing;
     - humility—the willingness to change and aware-
       ness that we need God's help;
     - renunciation—turning away from wrongdoing;
       deciding not to do it again
3. Ask God for forgiveness for what we have done
   wrong.
  a. we do this in many ways: as part of our baptismal
     vows which we reaffirm during the penitential
     rite at Eucharist; through the prayer before Com-
     munion, "Lord, I am not worthy to receive you,
     but only say the word and I shall be healed";
     and within the Sacrament of Reconciliation
  b. make forgiveness a part of our relationships with
     others

In the Apostles' Creed, we say:
**I believe in ... the forgiveness of sins, ... and
the life everlasting.**

4. The Church also offers us guidelines for the formation of conscience in accord with the Good News
   of Jesus, the Ten Commandments and the teaching of the Church. Scripture offers us some lists of
   specific kinds of wrongdoing: spiritualism, witch-

craft, occultism, sex outside of marriage, adultery, homosexual acts, murder, robbery, stealing, cheating (business deals, on exams), lying, slander, and self-abusive acts

- Those who are in the state of serious sin need sacramental confession as part of the process of reconciliation. Sacramental confession can also be very helpful for those who have not committed serious sins, but who are turning to the Lord in a new way.

C. As we turn toward God and surrender our lives, then the Spirit fills us with new life. There is a vast and endless river of life that gives us a new birth in Christ. Next week we will pray for a deeper experience of baptism in the Holy Spirit, who is living water.

1. Jesus sends us the Spirit like he did on the first Pentecost

"When the Holy Spirit comes upon you, you will be filled with power, and you will be witnesses for me in Jerusalem, in all Judea and Samaria, and to the ends of the earth." (Acts 1:8)

2. The Catholic understanding of receiving the Spirit also involves the Sacrament of Confirmation, which is a "personal" Pentecost. The *Catechism of the Catholic Church* calls Confirmation "the special outpouring of the Holy Spirit as once granted to the apostles on the day of Pentecost" (CCC # 1302). A new and stronger flame of God's energizing presence is given. Any one who has not been confirmed, may want to pursue receiving this sacrament in order to be fully initiated into the Spirit. Prayer for release of the Spirit does not take the place of the Sacrament of Confirmation.

CONCLUDING REMARKS

Next week there will be an opportunity for each person to pray for baptism in the Spirit.

A. Explain the format of Session 5. We will prepare for a release of God's Spirit by:
   1. Calling upon our loving Father in prayer, focusing on Jesus, who is Christ and Lord, asking him to send the Holy Spirit (Luke 11:13). Surrender obstacles to receiving God's gifts and charisms—a feeling of unworthiness, fear of being foolish, doubts about God's love, temptations to reject God's gifts, pride and excessive self-reliance
   2. Renewing our Baptismal vows together (Remind them about the Commitment Prayer Handout or the "Commitment to Christ" in *Finding New Life in the Spirit*.
   3. Members of the community/prayer group will pray for each of you with the laying on of hands, asking for a new outpouring of the Spirit.

B. What we can expect as we pray together:
   1. An affirmation of the sacramental life in the Spirit, a kind of personal Pentecost: "They were all filled with the Holy Spirit and began to talk in other languages, as the Spirit enabled them to speak." (Acts 2:4)
   2. We can expect God to touch us with the power and presence of his Spirit in ways that are most suited to our own unique relationship with God.
   3. A variety of charisms, gifts and fruits of the Spirit will be given for the good of the Body of Jesus—experiencing the presence of God, peace and joy, tongues, prophecy.

COMMENTS ON THE PRESENTATION

The 1979 version of the seminar reminds us that there is a close connection between three things: belief (Mark 16:16), repentance (Acts 2:38), and baptism (Mark 16:16, Acts 2:38). They are like three strands that make a single strong rope. (Ecc. 4:12). An initial conversion or a renewal of one's commitment to the Lord will involve all three in some way. For someone who is just becoming a Christian, repentance means a total reorientation of life, faith includes an acceptance of basic Christian truths, and baptism means a sacramental baptism. For someone who is already a baptized Christian, deeper level of faith, repentance and immersion in the Spirit are possible. The graces of Baptism, Confirmation and Eucharist are renewed, redefined and released in the person's life.

Repentance, faith, baptism and surrender to the gift of the Spirit are all parts of the covenant that God has made with us. God gives us a desire to renew and deepen that covenant relationship in daily life. The Lord wants this even more than we do, so we can ask with expectant faith that God will release in us the power of the Holy Spirit that will renew us. It is the Lord who baptizes us in the Spirit.

In section A, we are offering a vision of surrender to God. We want to convey a real confidence in God, which allows us to abandon ourselves the way Jesus did. We are concerned with something that is very simple. For many this may be the first time they are taught to put faith first, to choose a life of faith, and not feelings. We want people to focus on Christ and his promises.

In section B we are offering a vision of conversion and repentance which are primary to the Christian life. We must turn toward God and cooperate with the gift to do so. In John, Jesus says "People can not come to me unless the Father who sent me draws them to me." (Jn. 6:44) Repentance also means openness to change and putting away anything which blocks a relationship with God. We are primarily concerned with any major things that are incompatible with the Christian life. We are concerned with things that obstruct the process of conversion and deeper growth in Christian life, therefore blocking baptism in the Spirit.

There are two kinds of repentance: basic repentance and advanced repentance. Basic repentance is concerned with "Big Sins," wrongdoing that is incompatible with Christianity. Paul gives a list of different types of such wrongdoing in 1 Cor. 5:11 and 6:9-10. There is another list in Rev. 21:9. Similar lists are scattered through out Scripture and based in the Ten Commandments. Advanced repentance, on the other hand, is concerned with faults that block our Christian progress, faults such as impatience, lack of prayerfulness, and gossip.

There are two reasons for centering on basic repentance in this talk. It is the starting point for many "unevangelized" people. Also, some people come to the Life in the Spirit Seminar with serious wrongdoing in their lives. At this point, it is important to get people into the right kind of relationship with the Holy Spirit so that they can be given a desire to do everything Christ wants. Once they start to fall in love with Jesus, they are ready for a more active discipleship and further repentance.

"Repentance" and "obedience" are closely related. Listening to God (a definition of obedience) and wanting to please God are important. If we are not listening, if we are doing something that God does not want us to do, we have to change. The Scriptures use the word "repentance" to describe that change. Repentance is not just feeling bad about what we have done (although that may be a part of it). It is an actual change of direction, a turning towards Jesus.

We want to mention common types of serious wrongdoing. Different groups of people may need different lists. When we talk about robbery, cheating, lying, etc., we are talking about activities of a serious nature. We are not talking about small offenses. Small offenses should also be done away with, but our concern here is to center on serious wrongdoing.

Section C offers Pentecost as a model for receiving the Spirit. It is important to bring up the Sacrament of Confirmation since a growing number of nominal Catholics are not fully initiated and the seminar can provide a conversion experience that will give them the impetus to pursue all the Sacraments of Initiation. Baptism in the Spirit can come at any point in the process of initiation.

The final announcement prepares people for the fifth session. It gives them a concrete idea of the way the session will look and how prayer for baptism in the Spirit will proceed. We should speak with confidence and faith, encouraging them to expect the Spirit is presence. (Remind them to reread leaflets, if they have them.)

Part II (F) Session 5: Praying for Baptism in the Holy Spirit

GOAL

To help people make an authentic commitment to Christ, through the renewal of baptismal vows and prayer for baptism in the Spirit. To encourage surrender to gifts and charisms of the Spirit. Hilary of Poitiers (c. 315-367) describes what did and can happen: "We who have been reborn through the sacrament of baptism experience intense joy when we feel within us the first stirring of the Holy Spirit. We begin to have insight into the mysteries of faith; we are able to prophesy and speak with wisdom. We become steadfast in hope and receive the gifts of healing."

The fifth week is a turning point in the seminar, a moment when many experience new life with Christ. It can be a real time of renewal and rededication. However, we should not approach the fifth week as if it were to be the culmination of a person's Christian life. Our attitude should not be, "This is it, we have reached the summit," but "Now let's get started." We want to convey the idea that it is the life in the Spirit, the life of following Christ, that is important, not the experience of discovering baptism in the Spirit for the first time. It is important to allow for all kinds of emotional responses, from crying to laughing to no emotions at all.

TEAM MEETING (BUSINESS) BEFORE THE FIFTH SESSION

1. Review last week's session
   - discuss any problems that appeared and what to do about them
   - go over the list of people and consider what should be done for them

2. Preview the fifth session
   • understand the goal (not just a spiritual experience,
     but a new relationship with Christ)
   • review the whole seminar paying attention to seating,
     tone, etc.

3. Discuss how to pray with people
   • how to help people relax, focus on the Lord
   • how to help them yield to tongues and other
     charisms, fruits and gifts—looking to the Lord for
     guidance

4. Pray for the seminar and the people in it

THE FIFTH SESSION

I. Brief introduction to the session
   - introduce any new people who have come to help
     A. The team leader gives a few brief instructions about
        the evening
        - prayer for surrendering obstacles and healing
        - Baptismal vows and the commitment to Christ
        - the laying on of hands and prayerful attitudes (done
          in faith-sharing groups)
     B. Explain how to yield to prayer charisms like tongues,
        visions, prophecy
     C. Important attitudes and directions

II. Prayer session in the large group
    A. Opening song and prayer
    B. Prayer of surrender to God (may add prayer for inner
       healing or Marian prayer)
       [TEAM OPTION: Mention Mary as a model of faith
       and as a participant at the first Pentecost. (See Luke
       1:26-38.) Mary was overshadowed by the Holy Spirit,
       and so Jesus became incarnate. Mary accepted a life-
       long call from God in obedience to the word that had

been spoken to her, (Cf. Luke 1:45, "Happy you are to believe that the Lord's message to you will come true.") Pray the "Hail Mary."]
- Conclude with asking the Lord's blessing and praising God.
C. Renewal of Baptismal vows **and/or** commitment prayer are recited together.
D. People adjourn to the same small groups they have had from the beginning. Faith-sharing group leaders and sponsors lay hands on each person, and ask the Lord to baptize each one in the Spirit. They intercede, encourage the person and listen for God's word.

III. When everyone is done the team leader draws the whole group together. A brief teaching on spontaneous praise and singing in tongues is given.
    A. Closing teaching and instructions:
        1. Different people have different experiences.
        2. Be aware that doubts and temptations are common.
        3. You can't expect all your problems to go away at once.
        4. Be faithful in daily prayer, especially praise and thanksgiving. Use new charisms in personal prayer, like inspired Scripture, tongues and prophecy. If you are involved in a community or prayer group, attend the meetings faithfully. Remind them to use their booklets.
        5. Be careful about sharing experiences with others.
    B. Concluding praise and worship in the large group. (End with Sign of Peace.)

COMMENTS ON THE DYNAMICS

The **team sets the tone** by centering on the Lord in prayer and praise. Faith "catches." In an atmosphere of spontaneous worship and lively faith, it is much easier to have faith. There should also be an atmosphere of peace and a relaxed joy. A quiet room or place should be chosen where there is the least noise and distractions. Those leading prayer should be warm and relaxed, conveying a mood of peace and calmness to those who are seeking baptism in the Spirit.

Section II A: The team should be free in the use of the spiritual gifts and charisms. The Lord will work through prophecy, words of wisdom, inspired Scripture, encouragement, discernment, tongues and healing, to name a few. If we are attentive to the prompting of the Spirit, and expect complimentary charisms to operate in the group, we will see God work in many ways that we might not have expected.

In addition to the important example of the team, the leader specifically encourages people to **yield to charisms**. It is important that people are open to any and all charisms for the sake of bringing God's love into the world. Paul said, "Make love your aim and earnestly desire the spiritual gifts."(1 Cor. 14:1) They are connected. We should expect Jesus to give gifts. We encourage people to cooperate with God by speaking out in faith and expecting God to give us gifts of praise. We do not want to place limits on what God can do with our minds, hearts, and voices. Mention praying in tongues as one of many means to growing closer to Christ. It is a common gift of prayer by which we can surrender our voice and thoughts to God, what Father Montague describes as a "spirit-language" that gives voice to our inner self before God. Those over fifty can compare it to hearing the "foreign" tongue of Latin at weekly liturgies.

Tongues may not be of first importance, when we consider charisms like healing, discernment, teaching, wisdom, encouragement, and hospitality, but it can be a gateway to the charismatic dimensions of faith. It gives a person a clear experience of being fully active in prayer, yet touched by the presence of the Holy Spirit. At the same time, we should make it clear that speaking in tongues is neither a necessary, nor certain, sign that a person has been baptized in the Spirit. We should encourage people to be open to all the gifts, charisms and fruits of the Spirit as they develop over time. We should not put so much stress on them that people's attention strays from Jesus.

In Section II C the renewal of our **Baptismal vows** or a commitment prayer to Christ make our desire for more of God's life very real and concrete, and grounds us in the Sacraments of Initiation. Just as we recite the creed together at Sunday liturgies, we now make a public statement of faith in the context of a community of faith and mutual support. This fosters and strengthens a person's decision to be a follower of Christ (Rm. 10:9).

The renewal of Baptismal vows brings people back to the roots of their faith by asking them to choose God, renounce evil, and unleash the power of that sacrament. Although this is a controversial point in the charismatic renewal, no other prayers of deliverance, either individual or communal are necessary. We believe in Jesus who is redeemer for all times and places. We are not talking about the kind of exorcism that is called for when there is reason to judge that an individual is actually possessed or obsessed.

Section II D—Praying with people: Some groups conduct the **prayer for baptism in the Spirit** in the context of collective, large group prayer, asking the Lord to release the Holy Spirit and give charisms. Within this format, small teams of two or three mature Christians pray over each person individually. Having a number of teams allows several people to be prayed with at the same time (avoiding long waits while others are being prayed with). Praying in twos provides communal support that is helpful. We would also highly recommend an alternate approach in which people adjourn to their small faith-sharing groups for this prayer, with the possible addition of a few guests in each group. Both methods are effective. The Lord will baptize people in his Spirit, whether the setting is primarily collective or primarily in small groups.

If the prayer will be done in small groups the atmosphere in the room should be prayerful. Encourage people to speak softly. The sound of prayer, or soft background music, provides privacy for those who are seeking baptism in the Spirit. Everyone in the room should be praying throughout the prayer session. The faith sharing leaders and sponsors should pray with those in their own groups. It is also appropriate to ask participants to pray with and "over" each other in these groups, since they know each other very well and need to begin to care for one another.

When praying with people for baptism in the Spirit we are primarily offering our encouragement and support in prayer. Some people will yield to the Spirit beautifully, others will need a little direction. Some need to be reminded that all sorts of emotions are possible and appropriate. After praying for a few moments ask a person what is happening. God will speak and act and they are equal partners in the endeavor. The Spirit will lead us and give us wisdom, Scripture, visions and prophecies to help them. Finish with a prayer of thanksgiving and praise.

After praying with a person for baptism in the Spirit, the team member should lean over or kneel down and ask the person if he or she would like to pray in tongues, or surrender to a particular charism. Guide that person and encourage him or her to pray with sounds (in order to receive tongues) or to share the words and images that seem to come to mind (for prophecy). The leader can say the same things that are in the opening remarks. The team member can often supply the faith that will allow them to yield to the Spirit through whatever charisms God is offering at the moment.

Section III—**large group closing prayer:** The team leader encourages people to pray and sing with whatever words and melody God gives them, whether it be a hymn or the gift of tongues. Singing in tongues is like speaking in tongues, except that the Holy Spirit also forms the melody. Many people find it to be an easier way to start. The leader encourages everyone to turn to Jesus and to begin to sing, yielding to the Spirit and allowing the Spirit to form the melody. (This kind of prayer was common place in the early centuries of the Church and was encouraged by St. Augustine. It persisted until the Middle Ages in forms called *jubilatio* and chanting.) Allow a few minutes at some point for people to surrender to prophecy, images and inspired Scripture. Ask them to share with a neighbor what they are hearing, then resume praise in the larger group. It may be appropriate to end with a prayer like the "Divine Praises" letting people respond to each line with spontaneous praise.

A Eucharistic celebration at the conclusion of the session is recommended in the 1979 edition of the seminar and is very appropriate. Just as the Sacraments of Initiation in the early Church concluded with the newly baptized joining in the Eucharistic celebration, it is fitting that the renewal of baptism in the Spirit conclude with a Eucharist. There are, however, practical reasons for not having a Eucharist during the same evening. Very often, there is not adequate time to do both well. Enough time should be taken to pray with people and give them the attention they need and allowing them enough time to respond to the Lord. Above all, the prayer session should not be ritualized, but people should be helped individually. It might also be possible to have a Eucharistic celebration at another time during the week.

EXPANDED OUTLINE OF THE SESSION

I. Introductory Explanation
 A. Jesus promises to send us the Holy Spirit (Jn. 14:16-17)
    "I will ask the Father, and he will give you another helper, who will stay with you forever. He is the Spirit, who reveals the truth about God."
  - Explain what will happen in the prayer session (mention the renewal of Baptísmal vows, commitment prayer, the logistics of how people will pray with them). Explain that the prayer session for the release of the Holy Spirit is modeled on the early Church's

ceremony for the initiation of Christians.
- Jesus baptizes us in the Holy Spirit and gives us God's own life. We will lay hands on you and pray with you as a sign of God's presence. Place yourselves in the presence and the love of Jesus.
- Different things will happen to different people.
- Do not seek a particular kind of experience. Just turn to the Lord and receive new life in the Holy Spirit.

B. How to yield to charisms
- We can expect and will receive many different charisms in a lifetime. These are gifts from God. Be open. We would never say to the Lord, "I want what you have for me except the gift of tongues, or prophecy, or almsgiving, or healing."
- Tongues is a gift of prayer that you may receive today, but do not expect the Holy Spirit to force you to speak in tongues. You yield to this gift by praying with sounds. We speak these sounds to God and the Spirit forms the words. "For we do not know how we ought to pray; the Spirit himself pleads with God for us in groans that words can not express." (Rms. 8: 26)
- After you pray for baptism in the Holy Spirit and ask for charisms, then yield to God in thanksgiving. Pray according to whatever God puts in your heart. Do not be afraid that it is just you, and not the Spirit. Do not be analyzing the sounds. Do not worry if you make sounds like babble or baby talk. There are lots of human situations that involve sounds beyond words. Make the sounds an act of worship to God. Focus on Jesus, not on the sounds. Pay attention to images and messages that seem to resound with God's presence. Share these with others. These words may be prophecies and are like a reply from God. Some will receive inspired prayers, images, Scripture passages, and feelings of peace, tears and joy. Yield to God in thanksgiving.

C. Some important attitudes:
   1. Relax. The more relaxed we are, the easier it is
      to receive the Lord's gifts. It is much harder to
      put something in a clenched fist than in an open,
      relaxed hand. The Lord loves you and wants you to
      experience his love in a new way.
   2. After we have prayed with everyone, we will gather
      in a large group to thank and praise God together.
   3. While you are waiting, pray for your brothers and
      sisters or praise God. We want an atmosphere of
      prayer to pervade the room until we are finished.

II. Prayer session in the large group
    A. Opening song and prayer

    B. Leader can help people surrender obstacles to God.
       Read Romans 8:28-39 and then ask them to give all
       their feelings, and any hurtful memories behind them
       to Jesus. Picture him coming into the situation and
       doing what is needed.

    C. OPTION 1 Renewal of Baptismal vows (lead by a priest
       or deacon if available):
       Do you reject sin, so as to live in the freedom of God's
       children?
       Do you reject Satan, father of sin and prince of dark-
       ness?
       Do you believe in God, the Father almighty, creator of
       heaven and earth?
       Do you believe in Jesus Christ, his only Son, our Lord,
       who was born of the Virgin Mary, was crucified,
       died and was buried, rose from the dead, and is now
       seated at the right hand of the Father?
       Do you believe in the Holy Spirit, the holy Catholic
       Church, the communion of saints, the forgiveness
       of sins, and the resurrection of the body and life
       everlasting?

OPTION 2 Commitment Prayer

Jesus, I know now that I am Yours and You are mine forever.

Thank You for sending Your Spirit to me that I might have the power to live this new life with You.

Stir up Your Spirit in me. Release Your Spirit in me.

Baptize me with the fullness of Your Spirit that I may experience Your presence and power in my life.

That I may find new meaning in your Scriptures.

That I may find new meaning in the sacraments.

That I may find delight and comfort in prayer.

That I may be able to love as you love and forgive as You forgive.

That I may discover and use the gifts you give me for the life of the Church.

That I may experience the peace and the joy that You have promised us.

Fill me with Your Spirit, Jesus. I wish to receive all that You have to give me.

Amen.

OPTION 3 Commitment prayer in *Finding New Life in the Spirit*

III. Closing remarks and prayer

    A. Different people have different experiences.

        1. Particular feelings and experiences are not the important thing. Look for the ways God is at work in you and respond to God's presence through gifts and charisms. If you did not speak in tongues or receive prophecy and healing tonight, do not worry about it! Do not make the mistake of identifying baptism in the Spirit with "getting the gift of tongues." In your prayer during this coming week, give plenty of time to praise and thanksgiving, aloud, if possible. But whether in tongues or with your own words, it is good to praise and thank Jesus for the gifts of the Spirit. If you find yourself

wanting to pray beyond words, then pray aloud
with sounds. Concentrate on God. Pay attention
to prophetic words and images. Use the Scriptures
to pray with, especially the Psalms.

2. Be aware that doubts and temptations can rob us
of God's gift of the Spirit. For Satan the next best
thing to keeping you from God is convincing you
that the gifts and the fire of the Spirit are not the
keys to life. Jesus is the way, the truth and the life.
Satan is just a defeated angel.

3. You can not expect all your problems to go away
at once. You need time to let God's love seep into
areas that are broken. The Holy Spirit will empower
you to look at what is needed and then learn ways
to be transformed.

4. Be faithful to a regular time of daily prayer and to
your local faith community. Pray with the charisms
you have received. "You have been faithful in man-
aging small amounts, so I will put you in charge
of large amounts. Come on in and share my happiness." (Mt. 25:21) What happened tonight is just
a beginning.

5. Go easy in sharing spiritual experiences with others.
It is possible to scare people off, to give them
more than they are ready for. The first thing to
do is to love them more than you did before and
serve them. The change in you will be a witness
to Christ. Go easiest with those who are closest
to you—especially your family. We will be talking
about how to share what we have found next week.
We will also be talking about how to grow in the
life of the Spirit. You need instruction on how to
respond to baptism in the Holy Spirit.

B. Concluding praise and worship (End with Sign of
Peace)

HELPFUL RESOURCES

Team Members may want to review one of several resources on the charisms:

More powerful Life in the Spirit Seminars by John and Therese Boucher audio series from CRS of LI, Inc. (Box 2151, Brentwood, NY 11717)

Pentecost Today (formerly called the *Chariscenter USA Newsletter*; Chariscenter USA, Box 628, Locust Grove, VA 22508-0628)

**** *Charisms: Stirring Up the Gifts of the Spirit* by Sr. Nancy Keller and David Thorp, a video series (Chariscenter USA, P O Box 628, Locust Grove, VA 22508).

Part II (G) Session 6: Growth

GOAL

To help participants make a commitment to grow in the life in the Spirit through prayer, community, Scripture and the sacraments. "I am the vine, and you are the branches. Those who remain in me and I in them, will bear much fruit; for you can do nothing without me." (Jn. 15:5)

The sixth week offers a vision of growth and maturity in our baptismal vocation as disciples of Jesus. Participants in the seminar are taught practical ways to make our life in the Holy Spirit something solid, something that will last. Although some will be familiar with the steps offered, they may need a fresh look at these in the light of a deeper conversion.

TEAM MEETING (BUSINESS) BEFORE THE SIXTH SESSION

1. Review last week's session
   - discuss any problems that appeared and what to do about them
   - go over the list of people and consider what should be done for them

2. Preview the sixth session
   - go over the goals of the faith sharing segment and the questions

3. Discuss how to help people who have had problems since last week
   - those who expected something other than what happened
   - those who have not yet experienced charisms like tongues, prophecy and healing
   - those who have run into some new problem or difficulty

4. Discuss how to help participants in the new phase (moving from the Life in the Spirit Seminar to an ongoing life in the Spirit)
   - encouraging them to make the commitments they need to make
   - helping them make connection with the community or prayer group
   - make **printed information** about any reunion, or future options for growth and faith sharing available this week and during the seventh session

5. Decide if a written evaluation of the seminar will be given to participants, or done through informal phone calls.

6. Pray for the seminar and the people in it

THE SIXTH SESSION

I. Introductory greeting and opening time of worship

II. Presentation
   A. We have several tools to help us grow in the life in the Spirit. It is important to choose the basic means to growth in intimacy with God, especially prayer, Scripture, study, community, the sacraments and service.
   B. We should spend time with the Lord through prayer, Scripture and study.
   C. We are called to be part of a sacramental, faith-sharing community.
   D. A Spirit-filled life includes many ways of sharing what we have found with others though service and evangelization.

III. Witness to **specific ways to grow**

IV. The Faith-sharing group
   Sharing: What kinds of spiritual gifts and struggles

have you experienced since last week? How have prayer, community, Scripture or sacraments sustained you in a relationship with God? What step could you take in order to grow more in the spiritual life? The leader can share his or her experience after others have answered.

V. Closing praise and worship

(Personal contact—during breaks and informal sharing team members should use the time to talk with anyone who seems to have a problem, or to make an appointment to get together with each person.)

COMMENTS ON THE DYNAMICS

The week after the fifth session brings a broad range of very different reactions and experiences for different people in the seminar. People will respond to the release of the Spirit with a whole range of emotions and thoughts. The most common reactions are—complete euphoria (the person has had an emotional and spiritual experience which includes a greater freedom and happiness than he or she has ever felt before); a desire of "I hope it lasts" (this person is already experiencing some doubts and fears that he or she may "lose it" if such a person is not careful); disappointment (a person's experience was not what he or she had anticipated, or he or she did not receive any noticeable charisms like praying in tongues); and a reaction that includes all of these feelings in a week (perhaps the most common category).

Each one of these reactions must be dealt with gently and lovingly. Team members need to convey understanding, compassion and a willingness to talk or pray about it with participants. The team must not squash euphoria or demand more from anyone than he or she can give. We must not brush off as unimportant or ridiculous anyone's disappointments or doubts. The sixth session helps people begin to integrate spiritual experiences with a deliberate approach to the life of the Spirit. Those who are disappointed, ecstatic and everything in between must be encouraged to an ongoing life of faith. We should help those experiencing the charisms and fruits of the Spirit to focus on serving the Lord. All should be encouraged to make the Word of the Lord their foundation.

(The faith sharing session) Sharing how the past week has been gives people a chance to see that they are not alone, whether their week was good, bad, indifferent. As people discover a common spiritual journey there is often a visible relief on some of the faces. Participants also learn to support one another. "Yes, I had that feeling too, this is what I did about it." Sharing group leaders and sponsors get a sense of where people are at, and what kind of help people need. People experiencing disappointments realize that these are normal. They aren't spiritual failures. Another goal of the session is to encourage participants to accept the many means of sustaining God's life that Jesus offers us. In this way we can bring together the many different gifts and spiritual experiences into the one Body of Christ.

EXPANDED OUTLINE OF THE PRESENTATION

II. Presentation

   A. We have several tools to help us grow in the life in the Spirit. It is important to choose these basic means to growth in intimacy with God, especially prayer, Scripture, study, community, the sacraments and service.
      1. Baptism in the Spirit is an ongoing reality, an ongoing process that involves time and attention like a houseplant, a grapevine or a huge tree. The Spirit is like the sap pulsating through the vine and each part of it. Jesus says "I am the vine, and you are the branches. Those who remain in me and I in them,

will bear much fruit; for you can do nothing without me." (Jn. 15:5) We must let the Spirit flow in
us.

2. In order to grow, each of us needs certain practices
   in our lives: prayer, study, service, and community.
   These are like spokes on a wheel. All are important.
   a. The power that comes from the Holy Spirit
      makes us grow like vines.
   b. We need to seek intimacy with God in these
      ways, so we are strengthened.
   c. Prayer, study, service and community are means
      to growth, ways of staying in contact with
      Christ.

3. The Christian life is not something we live alone,
   but in community. God has made a covenant with
   us and with centuries of believers. Our life in Christ
   calls us forward together. "We have this large crowd
   of witnesses around us. So then, let us rid ourselves
   of everything that gets in the way ... and let us run
   with determination the race that lies before us."
   (Hb. 12:1)

B. We should spend time with the Lord through prayer,
   Scripture and study.

   1. Personal relationships (friendships) flourish when
      people spend time together. Our relationships with
      God need **regular** amounts of time to grow also.

   2. We can imitate Jesus in the way he set aside time to
      go to "a lonely place" and be revived by the Spirit.
      Jesus wants to speak to us, to be with us, to heal
      and revive us as we pray. Prayer is like stepping
      out of clock time and into the fullness of time. St.
      Therese of Lisieux says, "For me, prayer is a surge of
      the heart; it is a simple look turned toward heaven,
      it is a cry of recognition and of love, embracing
      both trial and joy. [It is a vast supernatural force
      which opens out my heart and binds me close to

Jesus.]" (See no. 2558 in the *Catechism of the Catholic Church*.)

3. Set aside time **every day** for prayer and Scripture reading.
   - decide on a particular time, a place, and some material to start with
   - do not be discouraged if you fail, just start over again the next day
   - consider keeping a journal, a set of "notes and letters" to God and responses (prophecies) from God.
   - use praying in tongues, psalms, or Scriptural titles for Jesus as a way to begin
   - if you want to follow the daily readings of the Church, there are at least three possibilities:

   - • *Living With Christ* published by Novalis (1 800 387 7164)
   - • *Share the Word* by the Paulist National Catholic Evangelization Association (3031 Fourth St. Wash., D.C. 20017-1102 or e-mail at pncea@pncea.org)
   - • *The Word Among Us Magazine* (P.O. Box 3646, Washington, D.C. 20007)

   (Include personal example of the value of a daily prayer.)

4. Many people experience greater depths of prayer as they combine it with studying Scripture and Church teaching. We need to let our minds grow in the Lord also.
   - studying Scripture helps us become aware of the unity of the whole Bible, gives us a context for any one passage or book, and can help us grow in discerning God's voice.
   - magazines might include: *God's Word Today Magazine* (Box 64088, St. Paul, MN 55164)

C. We are called to be part of a sacramental, faith-sharing community. The Church acknowledges how vital
this need is by asking us to participate in Sunday liturgies.
   1. God brings together a people. Pentecost brought
   about the creation of a community of Christians
   (Acts 2:41-47). Pentecost is the birthday of the
   Church.
   - Community is not an optional extra, it is essential
   to the life of the Spirit.
   - Body of Christ for the salvation of the world.
   - This is why (in our creed) we say:
   **I believe in the holy Catholic Church and the
   communion of saints.**

   2. We are invited to belong to the Church community on many levels:
   - Jesus touches us through the sacraments. Baptism,
   Confirmation and Eucharist are the gateway to a
   sacramental life. Eucharist is the ordinary way to
   meet the Lord. During the liturgy we call on the
   Spirit to consecrate both the bread and those gathered into the Body of Christ. Other sacraments offer
   healing and strength for the life and vocation God
   has called us to. All this is accomplished through
   the Spirit at work in the Church. "Sacraments are
   'powers that come forth' from the body of Christ
   which is ever-living and life-giving." (CCC, no.
   1116)
   - Most of us need a small faith-sharing group where
   we can share personal experiences in following
   Jesus. To grow in the life of the Spirit we need to
   get together with Christians who have experienced
   the same thing we have.
   - Large charismatic gatherings of Catholics will help
   us broaden and celebrate the Spirit alive in the
   Church.

3. Explain how to make contact with the parish, small faith sharing communities or prayer groups. (Mention regional meetings and conferences too.)

(Include personal example of the value of community.)

D. A Spirit-filled life includes many ways of sharing what we have found with others through service and evangelization. God sets our hearts on fire, like the disciples on the road to Emmaus. "They said to each other, 'Wasn't it like a fire burning in us when he talked to us on the road and explained the Scriptures to us?'" (Lk. 24:32)

1. God will give us a desire to share what Jesus has done in our lives. We call this a gift for evangelization. The U.S. Bishops define it as "bringing the Good News of Jesus Christ into every human situation and seeking to convert individuals and society by the divine power of the Gospel itself ... proclamation and response of the person are both the work of the Spirit." (*Go And Make Disciples*, page 10)
   - With friends and family we should begin with concrete acts of love that they can appreciate.
   - Watch for people who are open to hearing our faith story, but avoid being too pushy, especially about a response to the Lord.

2. Sharing the Good News also means serving all kinds of needs in those around us—what can be called spiritual and "corporal" works of mercy enlivened by the Spirit of God (providing food, clothing, shelter, encouragement, and interceding for needs; speaking out for Gospel values, working for peace and justice in society.)

Pope John Paul II summarized this challenge to grow in speaking to lay renewal groups on March 1,

1999. He said that questions every Christian must
ask are:
"What have I done with my Baptism?... My Con-
firmation?
Have I made the gifts and charisms of the Holy
Spirit bear fruit?...
Is my marital, family and professional life imbued
with Christ's teaching?...
What contribution do I make to creating ways of
life more worthy of man and to inculturating the
Gospel amid the great changes taking place?"

COMMENTS ON THE PRESENTATION

The Christian life can be compared to a bicycle wheel.
The rim of the wheel represents the Christian's daily life.
The hub of a wheel is the source of power and direction
for the whole wheel. It holds the wheel together. The hub
of the Christian life is Christ himself (at the center, the
heart). In order to transmit the power and direction from
the hub to the rim, spokes are needed. Some spokes in the
Christian life are prayer, study, service, sacraments, and the
many forms of faith community. These are means to put
our whole life in contact with Christ, so that each one is
transformed and enlivened by the power of the Spirit of
Jesus.

The purpose of the wheel imagery is to focus on basic
means of growth, and the need for a balanced life that
includes these. It is important not to try and explain each
of these in detail, but to inspire people to choose a full life
of faith. We want to encourage people to participate in and
grow in the life in the Spirit in these ways. Encourage them
to choose one area at a time that may need attention, and
work with the others later.

Section B is meant to encourage people to pray. Daily
prayer is a good goal to foster. It can be a simple presen-

tation, but should include personal examples. The speaker should describe several different ways to pray so participants can get a feel for the multitude of possibilities. It would be good to mention Scripture as a companion to prayer and as a source of understanding God. Studying within the Church will give us a foundation from which we can discern individual insights, charisms and gifts from the Holy Spirit.

Section C provides a vision of normal Christian life as being a communal one. Encourage people to realize their need for other Christians as part of an ongoing effort to grow. In this section we stress the fact that community is part of God's plan and based in our human nature. We need community that is "little, large, and liturgical." Jesus provides sacramental encounters and celebrations for all the important moments in life. The speaker can share how community has been of personal value. Some Catholic parishes foster small communities in which people can share their lives with one another. Prayer groups and large regional charismatic meetings fill still other needs. We want to encourage people to an active sacramental life, knowing that this idea may be new to many people. Recommend resources and local people who can help. It is not necessary to encourage involvement in many church activities. Many will, in fact, need to cut down on the activities in their lives. We encourage them to seek the right kind of involvement for growing in the Lord.

Some who experience a release of the Spirit, especially if they have not been active in the Church before, may experience a disappointment in the Sunday liturgy or even weekday liturgy. The liturgy is meant to be an important part of our spiritual life, but it may take time to integrate a new vision of spontaneous, charismatic worship with prayer that is ritualized. There are steps we can take to understand and grow in this area. There is so much more to learn. It is up to us to convey excitement about learning!

In Section D we want to do two things: 1) explain what evangelization is in terms of what has happened to people, and 2) convey a vision of evangelization that includes both freely sharing about God, and works of loving service empowered by the Spirit. The desire to share faith will be a new gift for many. Encourage them to use it in moderation. Coming on too strong or too hard or too fast can be harmful, especially to those who are close to us. Proceed carefully. When we love others, we will want to share the Good News! It will be a natural overflow of our new life. Our first concern is to work on the quality of our relationships. This is the context of what we say. Friends and family need to know that we love them. Once they experience something new in us, they will be more open to listen. Those who are close to us can be threatened easily. People react in different ways to what we share with them about our new life in the Spirit. When our relationship with someone is bad or problematic in some way, it is usually good to go slow. We can be freer when we have a close, warm, trusting friendship with someone. The Spirit who set the fire of God's word within us will lead us.

Part of proclaiming Jesus is the service we offer, not only to those around us, but through actions that "foster gospel values in our society, promoting the dignity of the human person, the importance of family, and the common good of our society, so that our nation may continue to be transformed by the saving power of Jesus Christ." (*Go and Make Disciples*, page 18) We are called to find ways to act out the gospel according to our vocation, our profession and our abilities. Again, the Spirit will lead us forward and increase the fruits of his presence in our actions: love, joy, peace, patience, kindness, goodness, generosity, gentleness, faithfulness, modesty, self control and chastity.

HELPFUL RESOURCES

During the sixth session, the team members might help **participants** choose prayer and resources that will help them grow in faith.

Books could include: *Reading Scripture as the Word of God* by George Martin (Servant, 1997)

Speak Lord, Your Servant is Listening by Msgr. David Rosage (Servant, 1987)

Being Catholic Today by Bert Ghezzi (Servant, 1997)

Understanding the Charismatic Gifts by Rev. Peter B. Coughlin (Bread of Life Renewal Centre, Box 395, Hamilton. ON L8N 3H8 Canada

The Ministry of Evangelization by Susan Blum (Liturgical Press, 1988) *Mother Teresa: Her Life, Her Works, Her Message* by Jose Louis Gonzalez-Balado (Liguori, 1997).

**** *Pentecost Today* (formerly called *The Chariscenter USA Newsletter*; Chariscenter USA, Box 628, Locust Grove, VA 22508-0628)

Dove Leaflets: #15 *Learning How to Pray* by O'Rourke, #62 *Hints for New Bible Readers* by Scully, and #3 *So You've Been Baptized in the Holy Spirit? What Next?* by Geraets.

Team members: **** *The Holy Spirit, Lord and Giver of Life* by the Theological-Historical Commission for the Great Jubilee of the Year 2000 (Crossroad Herder Book, 1997) or *Come Holy Spirit: How to Help Your Parish Grow in the Holy Spirit* by Karen M. Herrmann (Bon-Fire Press, 136 Vireo Drive, Wintersville, OH 43953)

Part II (H)
Session 7: Transformation in Christ

GOAL

To offer a vision of ongoing transformation that includes a strong spiritual identity and a sense of mission. To exhort participants to persevere as part of the Body of Christ so that they can bear fruit, despite the trails that they may experience. "You did not choose me; I chose you and appointed you to go and bear much fruit, the kind of fruit that endures." (Jn. 15:16)

The final session is a combination of two things: more instruction on how to grow in the Christian life and direction on how to serve the Lord through new found spiritual awareness and gifts. There is so much more to come! The last session can be a time of working through difficulties, making commitments to go on, but is mostly a time of encouragement.

TEAM MEETING (BUSINESS) BEFORE
THE SEVENTH SESSION

1. Review last week's session
   • discuss any problems that appeared and what to do about them
   • go over the list of people and consider what should be done for them

2. Preview the seventh session
   • go over the goals to be achieved, the faith sharing questions, and the ways that people will be invited to future community events

3. Pray for the seminar and the people in it

THE SEVENTH SESSION

I. Greeting and introductory prayer

II. Presentation (at least the fourth part should be given by the team leader)

  A. The Holy Spirit is at work to transform us and make us holy

  B. The gifts and charisms of Spirit help us carry on the mission of Jesus.

  C. Trials and difficulties are a normal part of the Christian life cycle.

  D. Persevere in the life in the Spirit within the Body of Christ.

  Explain opportunities for growth and service and ways to keep up contact with the parish community or prayer group.

III. Witness to **mission and ministry**

IV. Faith-sharing group

  Sharing question: What do you think holiness means in everyday life? How is God calling you to be a "missionary" within your own family, parish and community? What charisms might be involved in this mission? How would you want to stay in touch with people in the Seminar after it ends? (Some teams give a short written evaluation form to participants at this time.)

V. Commissioning and Concluding Prayer of Thanksgiving

EXPANDED OUTLINE OF THE PRESENTATION

II. Presentation

    A. The Holy Spirit is at work to transform us and make us holy. The Spirit is drawing us into a deeper union with God and one another, always offering us a fuller experience of new life.

        "Offer yourselves as a living sacrifice to God, dedicated to his service and pleasing to him. This is the true worship that you should offer. Do not conform yourselves to the standards of this world, but let God transform you inwardly by a complete change of your mind. Then you will be able to know the will of God—what is good and is pleasing to him and is perfect." (Rms. 12:1-2)

        1. Our primary identity is as bearers of the Spirit, children of God, and followers of Jesus Christ, our Lord (not in social position, job, astrological signs, or appearance)

        2. We must find more and more ways to be holy and to turn away from wrongdoing, to reorder our priorities, to serve God. Conversion can be emotional (our feelings), intellectual (our minds), moral (our actions), and socio-political (our stance toward the world). Every part of life needs the light of the Spirit.

        3. Every one around us needs to experience the **fruits** of the Spirit from us—love, joy, peace, patience, kindness, generosity, self-control. Include personal example of how the Lord transforms us.

    B. The gifts and charisms of the Spirit help us carry on the mission of Jesus.

        Jesus said to his disciples, "The harvest is large, but there are few workers to gather it in. Pray to the owner of the harvest that he will send out workers to gather in his harvest." (Mt. 9:37-38) The (**sanctifying**) **gifts** of the Spirit will transform the ordinary tasks we do—wisdom, understanding, piety, awe towards God, fortitude....

1. We are given a combination of both natural talents and charisms to enable us to serve the Lord and his people. Take time to discover what God is offering you and how you fit into the orchestra of charisms that function in a faith community.
   - Look at the lives of the saints for examples of how to manage charisms.
2. Learn more about **charisms** and let them unfold over time for the sake of the Church and the world: administration, celibacy, craftsmanship, discernment, evangelism, encouragement, faith, giving, healing, intercession, interpretation of tongues, knowledge, leadership, mercy, inspired music, prophecy, teaching, praying in tongues, voluntary poverty, and wisdom.

C. Trials and difficulties are a normal part of the Christian life cycle.
1. The Lord can use them for our growth.
   - "God works for the good in everything with those who love him." (Rm. 8:28)
   - Spiritual writers talk about a cycle that imitates the Paschal Mystery of Jesus. When we follow him we also die, then rise, then receive the Spirit, then die, rise.... Another description of this cycle involves honeymoon, followed by disillusionment, then a new and more balanced reality.
   - St. Ignatius of Antioch entered a Roman arena saying, "I am God's wheat and I am ground by the teeth of wild beasts that I may be found pure bread of Christ."
2. We now have a new power to deal with difficulties.
   - The Lord will teach us things through overcoming difficulties. St. Alphonse Liguori said, "He who trusts himself is lost. He who trusts in God can do all things."

- We are called to joy and thanksgiving as a way of life. (1 Thes. 5:16-17)

3. Help is available from the members of the community, especially those more mature in the life of the Spirit.
(Include personal example of how a difficulty can be overcome.)

D. Persevere in the life in the Spirit within the Body of Christ.

Explain opportunities for growth and service, as well as ways to keep up contact with the parish community or prayer group.

1. We need to learn more about the Christian life and continue spiritual formation
- Take advantage of the teaching, which is available in the community.
- Find ways to grow in union with the Church as we strive to be the People of God, the bride of Christ, temple of the Holy Spirit, the Vineyard and the New Jerusalem.

2. We need the strength and support of others, the sharing of experience, advice
- A good way to put out a fire is to pull the logs apart, a good basis for starting a fire is to put them together in the right way.

3. We need situations in which we can learn how to serve the Lord.

COMMENTS ON THE PRESENTATION

The seventh session, like the sixth, is an instructional session. Many people, even at this point, still think that once baptized in the Spirit, nothing can go wrong. They are on a spiritual honeymoon. Often for such people, the first setback can destroy their faith. The seventh session makes it clear that they should expect difficulties and that those difficulties can be a source of great advance.

The seventh session should convey a sense of the power and victory of the Lord. Difficulties come. But the Lord has given us the power of the same Spirit that raised Jesus from the dead. God is setting us on the path of holiness and transformation. We do not have to be fearful. We are in God's hands, and the Spirit will be faithful. God wants to make us new men and women.

The seventh session is also a time to convey the vision of mission as a vital part of our baptismal life in Jesus. Fruits, gifts, and charisms become tools for witnessing and furthering the Kingdom of God in our midst. Be careful not to treat them like a shopping list, but more like Christmas gifts that God gives us. Again, we ask people to choose one step in the journey of transformation and service within the Body of Christ. We encourage a definite commitment to a definite community and service. They are welcomed and needed. In some ways this is the most important part of the talk. If the people in the seminar do not make the commitment to go on with others, they will probably not be able to go on nearly as well.

The first two parts of the talk should be given with personal examples. The more it is presented in an experiential way, the more effective it will be.

Section A: Jesus wants us to enter into a deeper relationship with him every day. He wants us to become as he is, more and more holy and perfect. But how can anyone make himself holy and perfect as God is holy and perfect? He can't. God himself must bring about our holiness and perfection, and he will if we let him. "God is at work in you, both to will and to work for his good pleasure." (Phil. 2:13) "May the God of peace sanctify you wholly; and may your spirit and soul and body be kept sound and blameless at the coming of our Lord Jesus Christ. He who calls you is faithful, and he will do it." (I Thes. 5:23-24) Just as Jesus is the one who redeems us and baptizes us in the Holy Spirit, so too is God the one who perfects us. There is no part of our lives that Jesus does not want to perfect. We must, for our part, allow Jesus to show us our imperfections and allow him to change us.

Section B: God will also show us our talents and gifts for the building up of the Church and for the evangelization of the world. No charism works well by itself. Rather it is a piece of a larger puzzle, a larger plan for bringing about the Kingdom.

Section C: Problems, difficulties and trials must be seen as opportunities for the grace of God to triumph. The Lord has given us a new power, and that power is at work in every situation. Problems like doubts, fears, lack of trust, self-pity, temptation; difficulties like distractions and dryness in prayer, mistakes in following the leading of the Spirit, and trials like persecution or misunderstandings are commonly experienced in these weeks. Some of these are simply part of an adjustment to new spiritual experiences that take time. The Church has centuries of wisdom we can draw upon. (See items # 731, 736, 800, 1831, 1832 and 2003 in the *Catechism of the Catholic Church*.)

Section D: During the last section of the talk the speaker (team leader, if possible) should express confidence in the participants and what God is doing in their lives. The people in the seminar also need to be aware of options for further growth, and information about concrete steps they can take. The team leader should explain ways the people in the seminar can be part of the community, parish, or prayer group for their own growth and in order to serve others. "You need to be part of the Church, and this is how you can be part of this one." Sometimes advice will be to come to a weekly prayer meeting. Sometimes more will be involved, whether it will be a reunion or a workshop. Whenever possible, **give the participants printed information** that includes a contact person's phone number. It is good to let someone invite people to such events during a break.

COMMISSIONING AND CLOSING PRAYER

A. It is important to cultivate an ongoing desire to receive a further outpouring of the Spirit, and a desire for the gifts and charisms most needed by the Church. Ask people to choose a partner. Ask them to share what gifts they need to serve God. Read Mt. 28:16-20 about the Great Commissioning and ask people to pray for their partners to receive the Spirit. This can be done in silence or aloud.

B. You might use a prayer to conclude the praying in twos:
Come, true light. Come, eternal life. Come, hidden mystery.... Come, light without sunset. Come, infallible hope of all who must be saved. Come, awakener of all who sleep. Come, resurrection of the dead.... Come, eternal joy. Come, incorruptible crown.... Come, my breath and my life. Come, consolation of my poor soul. Come, my joy, my glory, my delight forever." (Simeon the New Theologian, Hymns, 949-1022)

C. Next, invite everyone to praise God together in the larger group. Ask the Spirit for the charisms most needed by the local church and the geographic area it serves. End with a time of thanksgiving and praise. Be sure to thank all the team members, musicians, teachers and hospitality people.

HELPFUL RESOURCES

Participants may want to consider:

Growing in the Fruits of the Spirit by John Blattner (Servant, 1984)

**** *Following Jesus: A Disciples Guide to Discerning God's Will* by John Boucher (Dove, 1995)

Becoming More Like Jesus by Bert Ghezzi (Our Sunday Visitor, 1987)

**** *Hearts Aflame* by Alan Schreck (Servant, 1995)

The Poor and the Good News by Tom and Lyn Scheuring with Marybeth Greene (Paulist, 1993)

Called and Gifted for the Third Millennium (Reflections of the U.S. Bishops on the Thirtieth Anniversary of the *Decree on the Apostolate of the Laity* and the Fifteenth Anniversary of *Called and Gifted*) (United States Catholic Conference, Wash. D.C. 1995).

PART III: APPENDICES

Part III (A) Use of Evaluations

It is important to ask both participants and team members about their experience of the seminar. This can be done verbally and/or in writing.

The most important questions are:
- What did you find to be **most helpful** during the seminar?
- What could have been **done differently** or was difficult for you?

These same two questions can be asked specifically about talks, prayer sessions, faith-sharing groups, facilities, contact with team members.

Part III (B) Concluding Team Meeting (Business)

GOAL: To get an overview of how the seminar went; to learn from the seminar

1. Go over the list of people and see what happened to them
    - Did everyone find a deeper relationship with Jesus? Were there difficulties in surrendering to charisms and gifts of the Spirit?
    - Was there something we could have done differently to help them find what they need to grow?
    - What did we learn from working with them?
    - Can we do something more for them this week or in the near future?

2. Go over the sessions
    a. the presentations
    - were they clear?
    - did they get the essential points across?
    - were they too long or too short?
    - what effect did they have on the people in the seminar?
    b. the faith sharing groups
    - was there a good spirit of openness and sharing in them?
    - did we accomplish what we needed to get accomplished?
    - what problems did we run into that we didn't know how to handle?
    c. personal contact
    - did we get it done?
    - were we able to address the needs that surfaced?

3. Share what the Lord did with us or taught us while we were working on these seminars—what was your

experience of the role/s you took?
- discuss long range possibilities for additional seminars
- set up a way to check on sponsors' ministry to participants: in one month, then two
- assign someone to compile written evaluations and write a report. The team leader should communicate the results of the evaluation to the people in the parish or community who have overall responsibility for the Life in the Spirit Seminar.

4. Pray for the seminar and the people in it: end with thanksgiving

5. Discuss the needs these particular people have for further growth. Consider offering a workshop using the *Catholic Spiritual Gifts Inventory* by Sherry Weddell (St. Catherine of Siena Institute, 5050 8th Avenue NE, Seattle, WA 98105-3603) during the coming year, or perhaps a short Bible study.

Part III (C)
Index of Materials by Title

title	week	team or par.	pg.
Faith Sharing within the Charismatic Renewal by Sr. Nancy Keller and Sr. Justin Wirth	Team	T	42
Fanning the Flame: What Does Baptism in the Holy Spirit Have to Do with Christian Initiation? ed. Rev. Kilian McDonnell, O.S.B., and Rev. George Montague, S.M.	Ex/One	P/T	48
Favorite Novenas to the Holy Spirit by Rev. Lawrence Lvasik	Three	P	113
Finding New Life in the Spirit: A Guidebook for the Life in the Spirit Seminars	One	P	47
Following Jesus: A Disciples Guide to Discerning God's Will by John Boucher	Seven	P	157
From Ashes to Fire: A Process for Lenten, Eastertime, & Pentecost Evangelization	Team	T	71
Go and Make Disciples: A National Plan and Strategy for Catholic Evangelization in the United States United States Catholic Conference	Ex	T	18,81
God's Word Today Magazine	Six	P	48,142
Growing in the Fruits of the Spirit by John Blattner	Seven	P	157
Healing Mass Project by CRS of LI	Team	T	71
Hearts Aflame by Alan Schreck	Seven	P	157
Holy Spirit, Lord and Giver of Life	Six	T	148
Hungry for God by Ralph Martin	Two	P	100
Introduction to the Catholic Charismatic Renewal by John and Therese Boucher	Ex/Three	P	48,82
Living with Christ by Novalis	Six	P/T	142
Ministry of Evangelization by Sue Blum	Six	P/T	148
More powerful Life in the Spirit Seminars by John and Therese Boucher, CRS of LI	Five	T	136
Mother Teresa: Her Life, Her Works, Her Message by Jose Louis Gonzalez-Balado	Six	P	148

Part III (D) Goals of the Revision of the Life in the Spirit Seminars

GENERAL GOALS:

Make the seminars more effective in the context of renewal efforts in Roman Catholic parishes by making the manual more compatible with Catholic expression and theology. Update the thinking behind the Seminar to include insights from *Fanning the Flames*, the *Catechism of the Catholic Church*, plus catechetical documents dealing with adult faith formation and Sacraments of Initiation.

Update recommended resources.

Strive toward inclusive language in describing people.

Shift from a discussion model, which can have an intellectual focus to a faith-sharing model sensitive to many levels of religious experience and background.

Shift from greeters to sponsors — according to the Church's initiation process.

GOALS FOR PARTICULAR SESSIONS:

EXPLANATION	Shift from the 4 spiritual laws to the Apostle's Creed as the skeleton of the talk.
GOD'S LOVE	Retain the invitation to choose a relationship with God, which for some means discover, and for others, rediscover God's love given at baptism

SALVATION	Stress conversion as turning away from sin and towards Jesus. More is added about who Jesus is. Following him means living our Baptismal Vows
NEW LIFE	Baptism of Jesus as model for receiving the Spirit
RECEIVING GOD'S GIFT	Surrender to God. Choose Jesus as Lord. Be immersed in the Spirit. Discover Pentecost.
PRAYING FOR BAPTISM IN THE HOLY SPIRIT	Broaden the idea of surrendering to many charisms. Treating participants as equals in prayer.
GROWTH	Means of growth include more on sacraments, study, service and evangelization.
TRANSFORMATION IN CHRIST	Charisms as tools for mission. Commissioning prayer.

Part III (E) Glossary of Terms

Baptism in the Holy Spirit
A conscious breaking forth of the graces and power of the Holy Spirit already received in the Sacraments of Christian Initiation (Baptism, Confirmation and Eucharist). God offers an inner awareness that activates our spiritual lives and gives faith an added dimensions.

Catechumenate
A time of formal preparation for entry (or initiation) into the Church, which involves formation, worship, community life, study and certain rites. Catechumens are preparing for **Sacraments of Initiation** (Baptism, Confirmation and Eucharist). The whole process is sometimes referred to as "the RCIA" meaning Rite of Christian Initiation of Adults. A recent Pope referred to adults who have been through the celebration of these sacraments without any significant conversion experience or spiritual formation as "quasi-catechumens."

Catechesis
Teaching what God has revealed to humanity, especially in Jesus Christ. Transmitting the Church's lived experience of the Gospel so that others may appropriate it and profess it. The goal of **catechetical** activity is a meaningful and active faith.

Charisms
Free gifts of grace given by the Holy Spirit to the faithful. By these gifts the Spirit makes us able and ready to undertake various tasks for the evangelization, renewal, and upbuilding of the Church and the world. The phrase "gifts and charisms" is used to heighten awareness of how what was traditionally known as "sanctifying" gifts like wisdom and fortitude, as well as "fruits" of the Spirit such as joy and peace, are meant to go hand in hand with charisms. It is

important to keep in mind that the Holy Spirit IS the GIFT. The rest are descriptions of the Spirit's activity.

Conversion
The changing of our lives that comes about through the power of the Holy Spirit as we accept the gospel of Jesus Christ. It is meant to be a continuous process that occurs in the emotional, intellectual, moral and social areas of our lives.

Discernment of Spirits
A kind of supernatural instinct by which the church perceives the origins, either divine or not, of thoughts, messages and visions. It is most fully exercised as part of an ongoing process.

Evangelization
Bringing the Good News of Jesus into every human situation. Its essence is the proclamation of salvation in Jesus Christ and the response in faith, both being the work of the Spirit of God.

Gift of Healing
The charism by which people experience a new physical, emotional, psychological, or spiritual wholeness flowing from God's Spirit, and sometimes from placing hands on a person in prayer. Healing of memories involves the removal of pain from past hurtful experiences. Healing masses include a special time of prayer for wholeness along with the use of other charisms.

Praying in Tongues
Praying in tongues involves language of non-rational prayer and song. Praying in tongues is a way of surrendering voice, inner self and thoughts to God. Sometimes a message is spoken in tongues to a community and then "interpreted." Someone else experiences a sense of the meaning of the words, or is inspired to yield to the charism of prophecy.

Prophecy

Prophecy is speaking forth of a word or communication from God, a kind of private and meaningful message, or the charism by which pieces of what God is saying to an individual are offered for the benefit and discernment of the community.

Witness

Speaker shares how he or she experiences God at work in the details of life, a telling of personal faith experiences, conversion, healing, and insights, for the upbuilding of the community.

NATIONAL SERVICE COMMITTEE

The National Service Committee is a body of leaders in the Catholic Charismatic Renewal who work together "as discerners of the Spirit" to serve the Lord in "renewing the grace of Pentecost in the life and mission of the Church." (NSC Vision Statement)

Flowing from this vision is the National Service Committee's sense of mission:

> The mission of the National Service Committee of the Catholic Charismatic Renewal is to stir into flame the grace of Pentecost within and beyond the Church, to broaden and deepen the understanding that baptism in the Holy Spirit is the Christian inheritance of all, and to strengthen the Catholic Charismatic Renewal.

In simple terms the first phrase focuses, as does the Vision Statement, on the *grace of Pentecost*, recalling the prayer of Pope John XXIII and the Church prior to the Second Vatican Council, *"Renew your wonders in our day as if by a new Pentecost."* The *grace of Pentecost* is meant to capture all that we mean and have experienced in that personal conversion to the Lordship of Jesus Christ and the empowerment with the Holy Spirit (see *Fanning the Flame*, pp. 12-13, 14-15, 26-27). The Committee's mission is to stir that grace into flame in individuals, in the Church, and beyond the Church.

The second phrase focuses both on the work within the Renewal of deepening our understanding of baptism in the Holy Spirit, as well as the theological work within the Church of demonstrating baptism in the Holy Spirit as integral and normative to Christian initiation and "as the power of personal and communal transformation with all the graces and charisms needed for the upbuilding of the Church and for our mission in the world." (*Fanning the Flame*, p. 27)

Finally, the third phrase addresses the continuing call of the National Service Committee to strengthen the Catholic Charismatic Renewal so that this grace of Pentecost will not be lost to the Church again, but indeed flourish in ever new and creative ways so that the Church as a whole and individuals will truly be renewed "as if by a new Pentecost."

NATIONAL SERVICE COMMITTEE
CHARISCENTER USA
RESOURCES

Bringing Christ to My Everyday World School of Evangelism
Nine half-hour interactive presentations such as "Whom Do I
Bring to Jesus?" and "How to Give Your Personal Witness."

3	90 minute videotapes and 10 workbooks	$54.95
5	60 minutes audiotapes and 5 workbooks	$29.95
	(Additional workbooks available)	

Catholic Charismatic Renewal Leadership Directory
An overview list of Renewal groups in the U.S. $5.00

Faith Sharing in Small Groups:
The Vision and the Tools (Revised)
Helpful material for small groups within Charismatic
Renewal as well as other parish groups including RCIA $5.95

Grace for the New Springtime
Pastoral Statement on the Catholic Charismatic Renewal.
(Call for prices)

Leadership Training Videotapes
- *Maintaining Vibrant Prayer Groups* $24.95
- *Charisms: Stirring Up the Gifts of the Spirit* $24.95
- *Service: A New Heart/A New Mind* $24.95
- *Unity: Building Relationships* $24.95
Each tape includes four presentations with a study guide.

Nurturing New Life in the Spirit: Training Sessions
for the New Life in the Spirit Seminar
Two video tapes and guidebook $34.95

All prices in U.S. dollars. Shipping and handling are extra.

Contact: National Service Committee
            Chariscenter USA
            P.O. Box 628
            Locust Grove, VA 22508
            (800) 338-2445
            Fax: (540) 972-0627
            E-mail: chariscenter@nsc-chariscenter.org

Pentecost Today

Pentecost Today is published four times a year by the National Service Committee. Formerly called the *Chariscenter USA Newsletter*, the new name expresses the Service Committee's Vision Statement: "renewing the grace of Pentecost in the life and mission of the Church."

SEMINAR LEADER

We would be happy to add participants in the Life in the Spirit Seminar to our mailing list to receive *Pentecost Today* for a year without cost. Please send us their names and addresses and we will gladly add them.

You may send the list by mail, fax or e-mail:

National Service Committee
Chariscenter USA
P.O. Box 628
Locust Grove, VA 22508
FAX: (540) 972-0627
e-mail: chariscenter@nsc-chariscenter.org

WORKSHOP:

HOW TO DO A NEW
LIFE IN THE SPIRIT SEMINAR

To fully understand and implement the vitally important changes in the Life in the Spirit Seminar in this Catholic Edition 2000, a workshop is available.

It is ideal for Seminar Teams from parishes and prayer groups, RCIA teams, sponsors and others interested in using this evangelistic tool to introduce people to a fuller experience of life in the Spirit.

For more information, contact:

National Service Committee
Chariscenter USA
P.O. Box 628
Locust Grove, VA 22508
(800) 338-2445
Fax: (540) 972-0627
E-mail: chariscenter@nsc-chariscenter.org